PLAY WITH FIRE

Discovering **FIERCE FAITH, UNQUENCHABLE PASSION,** and a **LIFE-GIVING GOD**

STUDY GUIDE | FIVE SESSIONS

BIANCA JUÁREZ OLTHOFF

ZONDERVAN.com

ZONDERVAN

Play with Fire Study Guide

© 2016 by Bianca Juárez Olthoff

This title is also available as a Zondervan ebook.

Requests for information should be addressed to: Zondervan, *3900 Sparks Dr., SE, Grand Rapids, Michigan 49546.*

Page design and layout: Crosslin Creative

ISBN 978-0-310-88070-7

First Printing July 2016 / Printed in the United States of America

CONTENTS

INTRODUCTION

Hi friend, I'm excited to be with you for the next five weeks! I know this sounds weird because we might not know each other, but I like you already. Why? Because if you're participating in this study, it probably means you are in need of a transformation in some area of your life. Maybe you feel like everything around you is up in flames. The good news is you're not alone. I've been there.

> *Play with Fire* was born out of a real and raw place in my life when I felt lost and lacking in almost every area. If you've read my book, then you know *exactly* what I'm talking about! Regardless of whether or not you've read *Play with Fire*, I'm excited for each one of you to walk through this video curriculum and study guide. Together, we will explore what it means to cry out to God, surrender our pain and confusion, embrace God's promises, learn the importance of taking part in genuine community, and experience the power of the Holy Spirit.
>
> Have you ever heard the story of the Phoenix—a well-known legend in Greek mythology? (If you haven't, I've included a shortened version for you before the first session because THAT is how much I love you.) When I read this story in college, I couldn't help but parallel the mythological creature's journey into the desert with my own. But even more, I found parallels with the biblical account of the Israelites journeying in the desert. So with my journal, my Bible, and my Greek mythology book all chronicling desert journeys and crying out for change, I saw that the desert was a place of transition and that fire was a powerful mode of transformation.
>
> My hope is this study guide and video lessons serve as a transformative experience for each one of you as Jesus meets you right where you are and brings you to a deeper place with Him, just like He did (and continues to do!) with me.
>
> Now that you understand the background, let's move on to study guidelines ...

STUDY GUIDELINES

> This is it. You have decided to be brave, and this is the beginning. As you go through each session, I want you to do the work. "The work," you ask? Yes, the work of digging deep into your soul and listening to the still, small voice calling you out

of your desert and into a new freedom. There is a land waiting for you where you can experience the fullness of God's promises. My hope and desire is that in the simple, you experience the profound; in the daily, you create a vision for the future; in the chaos, you experience God leading you to peace.

Here are some guidelines to help you get the most of this study and make the most of your time ...

- **Be willing.** If you want something in your life to change, something has to change (#DeepThoughts). But seriously, if you're taking the time to do this study—either by yourself or with friends—you need to be willing to open your heart to what God wants to do. I want this to be less about the daily homework and more about the daily willingness to go the distance and do the distance.

- **Do the work.** Here's the thing: it will take about twenty to thirty minutes of your day (including the extra credit) to do the homework for each session. I know, I know, that feels like a lot of time. But trust me, it's not. It's less time than a show on Netflix, less time than it takes to drink a coffee, and probably less time than your commute to work.

- **Commit to finish.** I get it. I really do. Starting is easy, but finishing is hard. However, when you cross the finish line knowing you jumped every hurdle, filled in every gap, and completed every page, it will be SO worth it. Not only do you get to say we finished the WHOLE study, but you also get a gold star in heaven. (Kidding!)

- **Sign it.** Yup, I am asking for your signature ... IN BLOOD! Just kidding. Go to the back of the book (the section titled "Your Commitment" on page 188) and write a note to yourself. Maybe it's a prayer of what you want to get out of the study. Maybe it's just a signed commitment promising to finish it. Either way, sign your name. You are going to thank your future self for making the promise that you would complete this study entirely.

- **Pray about it.** Pray and ask God to transform you over these next five weeks.

Before you continue, please know that I'm honored—no, I'm RIDICULOUSLY EXCITED—that you are committed to doing this study with me. This isn't something that I just threw together. Nope, this is something that I've lived out for seven years. Just as my life was transformed in the midst of fire, my hope is that your life will be changed as well. No longer are we slaves to things, people, or trauma that has kept us down. No longer do we have to wander in the wilderness. No longer do we have to sing songs to a sun that doesn't hear us. We have the privilege of crying out to God and knowing He hears us and will answer at the perfect time.

Now, let's move on to the group guidelines ...

HOW TO USE THIS GUIDE AS A GROUP

Note: This is all the smart stuff my editors want me to tell you about. So pay attention! Or not. No one is watching ... EXCEPT GOD. (Did I scare you? I hope so! Just kidding. Well, half kidding.)

Group Size

The *Play with Fire* video curriculum is designed to be experienced in a group setting such as a Bible study, a class during your weekend gathering, or a small group (in week five we will see that community is *muy importante*!). After viewing each video session, you and your group members will participate in a time of discussion. Ideally, discussion groups should be no larger than twelve people (unless it's a major rager, because those are always fun).

Materials Needed

Each participant should have her own study guide, which includes video outline notes, group discussion questions, and in-between personal studies to deepen learning between sessions. Participants are also strongly encouraged to have a copy of the *Play with Fire* book (all proceeds go to the FEED THE OLTHOFF CHILDREN fund). Reading the book alongside the curriculum provides even deeper insights that make the journey richer and more meaningful. A few quotes and excerpts from the book are in the study guide; however, they will make the most sense within the context of the book.

Timing

Each group session is timed for one hour. The time notations given—for example (19 minutes)—indicate the *actual* time of video segments and the *suggested* times for each activity or discussion. There are also suggested times in the in-between sessions sections for personal Bible study and individual activities.

Facilitation

Each group should appoint a facilitator who is responsible for starting the video and keeping track of time during discussion and activities (probably someone who likes Excel spreadsheets, color-codes her notes, and washes her hair everyday). Facilitators may also read questions aloud and monitor discussions, prompting participants to respond and ensuring that everyone has the opportunity to participate. Group *Ground Rules* are always a good suggestion too (basically, be nice, don't talk too much, and give people permission to speak freely).

Between-Sessions Personal Study

Maximize the impact of this series with additional study between the group sessions. As I mentioned before, finding time to spend with Jesus must be an intentional decision, so be deliberate and committed to each activity. Your time will include:

- **Scripture Reading.** Duh! This whole study is about the Bible, so be prepared to crack open your Word and get busy.

- **Personal Questions.** Reading the Bible is one thing, but taking personal inventory and assessment is another. Make sure you are evaluating the Word of God with the reality of your life.

- **Hebrew History.** The English language is quite limited when it comes to defining words. I've included a short section with original Hebrew words to help us understand the weight and depth of each daily activity.

- **Daily Activity.** There are all kinds of ways we comprehend and process information. Whether you journal, draw, pray, sketch, or sing, I really want you to have the opportunity to process, practice, and ponder what God is telling you each day.

- **Extra Credit.** This is my favorite section because I'm motivated to earn gold stars and excel at Bible trivia! (Don't judge. I'm competitive.) But seriously, this is a GREAT opportunity to dig deeper into God's Word and absorb even more biblical truths each day. Make sure you stretch yourself to do the hard work.

Please note: If you are unable to finish (or even start!) your in-between sessions personal study, still attend the group studies (even though I might secretly shake my head at you for watching reality television instead of doing your homework). We are all busy and life happens. You are still wanted and welcome in your group, even if you don't have your "homework" done.

Scripture Memory

Each session includes key Scripture verses that highlight the topic and themes. If you wish to maximize your learning experience, you may attempt to memorize these verses (especially if you want a big crown in heaven … I kid, I kid). It may be helpful to let your group facilitator know if you're attempting to memorize key verses. Perhaps those individuals will want to practice these verses with each other.

Fun

Have FUN! This series is designed to pair well with an inclusive atmosphere, delicious snacks and beverages, and a little hot sauce (because really, life is too short for it not to be spicy!). And get ready to *play with fire!*

So, fly on, Phoenix, fly on. You're almost home.

XO,

THE STORY OF THE PHOENIX

There is a bird that lays no eggs and has no young. It was here when the world began and is still living today, in a hidden, faraway desert spot. It is the phoenix, the bird of fire.

One day in the beginning times, the sun looked down and saw a large bird with shimmering feathers. They were red and gold—bright and dazzling like the sun itself. The sun called out, "Glorious Phoenix, you shall be my bird and live forever! Live forever!"

The Phoenix was overjoyed to hear these words. It lifted its head and sang, "Sun, glorious sun, I shall sing my songs for you alone!"

Almost five hundred years passed. The Phoenix was still alive, but it had grown old. It was often tired, and it had lost much of its strength. It couldn't soar so high in the sky, nor fly as fast or as far as when it was young. "I don't want to live like this," thought the Phoenix. "I want to be young and strong."

So the Phoenix lifted its head and sang, "Sun, glorious sun, make me young and strong again!" But the sun didn't answer. Day after day the Phoenix sang. When the sun still didn't answer, the Phoenix decided to return to the place where it had lived in the beginning and ask the sun one more time.

When at last the bird came to the place that had once been its home, it landed on a tall palm tree. The Phoenix sat down in its nest, lifted its head, and sang, "Sun, glorious sun, make me young and strong again!"

This time the sun heard the song. Swiftly it chased the clouds from the sky and stilled the winds and shone down on the mountainside with all its power.

Suddenly there was a flash of light, flames leaped out of the nest, and the Phoenix became a big round blaze of fire. After a while the flames died down. The tree was not burnt, nor was the nest. But the Phoenix was gone. In the nest was a heap of silvery-gray ash.

The ash began to tremble and slowly heave itself upward. From under the ash there rose up a young Phoenix. It was small and looked sort of crumpled, but it stretched its neck and lifted its wings and flapped them. Moment by moment it grew, until it was the same size as the old Phoenix. The young Phoenix lifted its head and sang, "Sun, glorious sun, I shall sing my songs for you alone! Forever and ever!"

"Now," said the Phoenix, "I must fly on alone." And while the other birds watched, it flew off toward the faraway desert. The Phoenix lives there still. But every five hundred years, when it begins to feel weak and old, it flies west to the same mountain. There it builds a fragrant nest on top of a palm tree, and there the sun once again burns it to ashes. But each time, the Phoenix rises up from those ashes, fresh and new and young again.[1]

FIRE

אֵשׁ

noun \ˈfī(-ə)r\

For our God is a consuming fire.
Hebrews 12:29 ESV

CRYING OUT

During that long period, the king of Egypt died. The Israelites groaned in their slavery and cried out, and their cry for help because of their slavery went up to God. God heard their groaning and He remembered his covenant with Abraham, with Isaac and with Jacob. So God looked on the Israelites and was concerned about them. **—Exodus 2:23–25**

INTRODUCTION: Dark Night of the Soul

At age twenty one, I was in the middle of a quarter-life crisis. My mom was diagnosed with brain cancer, I had a bad breakup with my boyfriend of three years, and I was a jobless college graduate living at home with my parents. I was the very definition of a crisis! I felt like the Phoenix bird in the desert, calling out to the sun, only to receive SILENCE. I was crying out, "God, where are you? God, what are you up to? God, please rescue me!" I was raw and weary and felt weighed down by pain, confusion, and desperation.

Looking back now, I see that my experience in those moments of pain and confusion was actually a Dark Night of the Soul. The fifteenth-century Christian writer John of the Cross was the first to describe this experience. He called it *La Noche Oscura*. Dark Nights often provoke deep questions spiritually and psychologically in our lives, and provide opportunities for growth.[1]

VIDEO TEACHING: Crying Out (21 Minutes)

Take a few minutes to play the video teaching for session one. As you watch, feel free to take notes or record any thoughts that stand out to you. Use the following concepts and questions to guide your group conversation.

NOTES

Name a time or season in life when you may have experienced a Dark Night of the Soul.

Based on our teaching, what does God say about our past?

And when you're alone there's a very good chance you'll meet things that scare you right out of your pants. There are some, down the road between hither and yon, that can scare you so much you won't want to go on.[2] —Dr. Seuss

DTR (Define the Relationship) = GOD + THE ISRAELITES.
Name a few things about God's relationship with the Israelites. How do we know God understood the pain of the Israelites during their wilderness journey?

Why is it important to voice our needs to God and for God?

A vital component in our relationship with God is VOICING our need for Him.
—Bianca

That is why, for Christ's sake, I delight in weaknesses, in insults, in hardships, in persecutions, in difficulties. For when I am weak, then I am strong.[3] —**The Apostle Paul**

What are your sorrows and pains? Where in your life are you crying out to God and asking Him, "Please deliver me!"?

What does Scripture show us about our weakness and God's strength?

In my distress, I called to the Lord; I cried to my God for help. From his temple he heard my voice; my cry came before him, into his ears.—**Psalm 18:6**

God HEARS
God REMEMBERS
God SEES
God KNOWS

The righteous cry out, and the Lord hears them; he delivers them from all their troubles.—**Psalm 34:17**

GROUP DISCUSSION (24 minutes)

Okay friends, now it's time to KIR [Keep It Real]! Our discussion will only go as far as we are willing to be honest. For us to have real change, we need to be real about where we are in our lives. Use these questions as a guide for group conversation:

{CONVERSATION STARTER}: Do you have a story about playing with fire as a kid or young adult? If so, share it with the group.

What stands out to you about the story of the Israelites' journey through the desert wilderness? What do you hear?

What is the difference between CRYING OUT and COMPLAINING? Share a few personal examples.

Like I always say, **"Honesty and vulnerability lead us to CRYING OUT." What keeps us from honesty and vulnerability as individuals and as a community? How can we encourage honesty and vulnerability as a community?**

God HEARS. When or how has God heard you?

On this adventure, don't fear the fire. Don't fear the invitation God is giving us to walk into transformation, and to experience the presence of God in those places where we feel this journey is a little scary, or a little dangerous. —**Bianca**

God REMEMBERS. How has God remembered you during a difficult season of life?

God SEES. What does it mean to be seen by God? How does this knowledge impact the way you live your life?

God KNOWS. Why do you think we try to hide things from God when the Bible tells us God is all-knowing? Name some of the ridiculous things we try to hide from God.

How does this teaching session change your perspective on life? Name at least one thing.

He knows that your past does not pre-determine your present. Your history does not determine your destiny. Your past is in your past because it's passed. —Bianca

GROUP ACTIVITY (10 minutes)

Take a few moments in your group to practice honesty and vulnerability *together*. Ask each person to SHARE (out loud) one specific area she wants God to transform in her. As everyone shares with the rest of the group, write down each person's answers in the space provided below, and then be mindful to pray for each person in your group this week.

GROUP PRAYER—CONVERSATION WITH GOD
(5 minutes)

Prayer is personal, and I would never require it to be forced, repetitious, or scripted. If you want to pray out loud your own unique conversation with God, go for it, homegirl! But if you need help forming language to communicate to God, I've included this prayer for you here.

God, we thank You for this group and for this session. Thank You that You hear us, You remember us, You see us, and You know us. Please help us to stop complaining and start crying out to You when we're in those desert moments of life. Please help us to practice honesty and vulnerability as individuals and as a group over these next few weeks. We believe You are the same God who rescued the Israelites in the wilderness, and we trust You will rescue us too. And we believe in Your power to TRANSFORM us as we learn to play with fire. Thank You that You choose us, and today, we choose You too. AMEN.

THANK YOU for being honest and vulnerable as individuals and as a group. God wants you to walk in freedom and fullness instead of wandering and complaining in the wilderness. And we are better when we walk in freedom together!

XO,

Then the LORD said, "I have surely seen the affliction of my people who are in Egypt and have heard their cry because of their taskmasters. I know their sufferings."
—**Exodus 3:7** ESV

DAY ONE
CRYING OUT

Embers of Silence

Voicing out loud our need for God is so vital in our relationship with Him and yet so countercultural to our Western world. Maybe you've grown up thinking that crying out is weak. Or maybe you think crying out is useless based on your own personal experience. Or you've been told crying out is only for people who really *need* the help. Reality check, homegirl: We ALL need help! In fact, Jesus straight up says, "Apart from me you can do nothing" (John 15:5).

Crying out to God is for ALL OF US. No matter how much pride or arrogance I try to hold onto, thinking I can do things on my own, I'm forced to cry out to God during situations that are overwhelming. I'm not alone in this.

What about Jonah? Do you think he just jumped into the belly of a whale? No! He was stuck and he cried out to God (see Jonah 2:1–10). How about Shadrach, Meshach, and Abednego? Did they just rely on their own superhuman strength to survive King Nebuchadnezzar's flaming fire? No! They cried out to God and believed God would come through for them (see Daniel 3:14–30). Or how about the disciples, stuck in a boat in the middle of the Sea of Galilee during a huge storm while Jesus was sleeping? (see Matthew 8:23–27)! Guess what—they cried out for help too.

These were defining moments for each one of these individuals: Moses and the Israelites; Jonah; Shadrach, Meshach and Abednego; the disciples; and now us. A "defining moment" is when something definitively changes in our lives—often inside and outside of us. Later in life, we look back on these moments and see that what follows is change ... or transformation. I refer to those moments as EMBERS OF TRANSFORMATION.

An *ember* is "a glowing fragment or smoldering remains of a fire."[4] It's the prelude to a dying fire or the precursor of a spark that can be fanned into a vibrant flame. An ember is the defining moment of a potential fire, and an ember of transformation is the defining moment of our potential lives. So let's embrace our defining moments—our embers of transformation—as opportunities given to us by God to PLAY WITH FIRE.

Personal Study (15 minutes)

 READ EXODUS 2:23–25. Think about the desert journey of the Israelites. Where are you now: entering the desert, in the desert, or an experienced traveler on the other side of the desert?

Describe a time in your life when you could relate to the Israelites. What did that season look or feel like?

Where do you currently feel stuck, worn out, tired, or in pain? How do you want to be rescued by God?

Where have you been complaining about life instead of crying out to God?

Call to me and I will answer you and tell you great and unsearchable things you do not know.[5] —**God**

 READ EXODUS 3:7–10. Fill in your answers to these statements regarding the Israelites.

- GOD HEARD:

- GOD REMEMBERED:

- **GOD SAW:**

- **GOD KNEW:**

How can you identify with this story of the Israelites?

What does God hear, remember, see, or know about you right now? What do you hear God saying to you?

Ask God to transform your complaining into crying out and your pointless wandering into purposeful walking. What are those cries to God? Where are you asking God, "TRANSFORM ME!"?

- **RELATIONALLY:**

- **SPIRITUALLY:**

- **PHYSICALLY:**

- **EMOTIONALLY:**

God heard their groaning and he remembered his covenant with Abraham, with Isaac and with Jacob.—Exodus 2:24

HEBREW HISTORY

UNDERSTANDING THE ANCIENT TEXT

GROAN:
a deep cry out

CRIED:
Hebrew word is tsaʻaq; with a loud voice from sorrow or fear

CRY:
*Hebrew word is shawaʻ; for help in distress;
it emphasizes the greatness of the distress*[7]

Hebrew letters for Crying Out:

Individual Prayer—Conversation with God

You're probably by yourself while doing your homework. This is the perfect time to practice praying out loud! There is something so powerful about verbalizing aloud your need to God. Think about trying to ask for directions without using words. Wouldn't that be difficult? I know God knows our innermost thoughts and knows all things (see Psalm 139:2, 4), but when we use our words to ask for directions, it proves we are brave enough to take the next step.

Use your own words to ask God to show you where you've been complaining and wandering instead of crying out and walking. Ask God to transform these areas of your life in ways that only He can do—with embers of glowing fire, embers of transformation. And then thank Him for this season of life—no matter how hard.

Individual Activity (10 minutes)

Take a few moments to practice SOLITUDE today. Find a quiet place and a comfortable position. Perhaps it's sitting at the beach, or in a chair in your backyard, or even in your car during school pick-up time. Maybe it's taking a few moments right now at your work desk or lying on your bed later this evening with your eyes closed and your heart open to receive what God says to you. Be still and focus your mind on God's presence with you. Listen. Don't ask or explain or talk—just LISTEN. Let God be with you in those moments.

What did you sense God saying to you in the midst of your solitude with Him?

What embers of transformation are apparent in your life right now?

What action steps do you need to take as a result of what you learned today?

Extra Credit (5 minutes)

We touched on the promises of God during session one, but I want to dig a little deeper if you have the extra time today. Throughout the transformational desert journey of the Israelites—all of the ups and downs, the grumbling, complaining, and crying out—God had to remind them of His promises and the covenant He had made with Abraham, Isaac, and Jacob. And, because of Jesus, those same promises hold true for us today. *So, how do you come back to the promises of God in the middle of a desert season?*

Listen to my prayer, O God, do not ignore my plea; hear me and answer me.[7]
—King David

Take a few moments to look up these verses and write down the **promises** you hear in these verses—the promises for the people in the Bible and the promises for us today.

EXODUS 33:12–14

DEUTERONOMY 31:6

ISAIAH 41:8–10

Are you tired? Worn out? Burned out on religion? Come to me. Get away with me and you'll recover your life. I'll show you how to take a real rest. Walk with me and work with me—watch how I do it. Learn the unforced rhythms of grace. I won't lay anything heavy or ill-fitting on you. Keep company with me and you'll learn to live freely and lightly.
—Matthew 11:28–30 MSG

GOD HEARS

The Invitation of Silence

Let's be honest for a moment: we think God's silence is an invitation to control our lives, our circumstances, and our relationships. *If God's not going to come through for us when we cry out to Him, then we will take care of it ourselves.*

Do you realize there was a 400-year period of silence between God and the Israelites during their time in Egypt? And we get upset over a four-minute delay when texting with our friends! Four hundred years—now that's a reality check!

I've learned over the years that God's timeframe is not always our timeframe, and I'm okay with that. I can accept it because I know it's part of the plan, part of the purpose for our lives. I'm okay with being in the desert because I know the desert is where we're strengthened and refined. It's where we gather courage and wisdom. But when there's a long period of silence in the middle of the desert, then I just want control of the desert terrain. I'm embarrassed to admit how natural it is for me to take control. And for a short period in my life, I saw God's silence as an invitation to take control.

Do you know how I did it? I said *yes* to everyone. Yes made me feel like I was in control of the outcome and that the results depended on me alone. "Yes" gave me the illusion that I could deliver joy and happiness to others, to myself.

But control is a manipulator. Control promises what it can't deliver. Control promises perfection. Ironically, I couldn't control myself out of my own desert, and the more I tried, the drier, hotter, and more desolate it became.[8]

Silence isn't God's attempt to push us further away. It's not His way of shaming or hurting us. It's not God's rejection of us. No, silence is God's invitation to us. And if you're Latino with a big, loud family like me, this may be a little strange. But silence is God's invitation for us to trust Him, to depend on Him, to wait patiently on Him. It's God's invitation for us to lean in, to be still, and to listen.

Personal Study (15 minutes)

 READ EXODUS 16:1–17. *Think about a time when you cried out to God and He heard you. Where were you? What were you doing? Why were you crying out to God?*

What happened as a result of God hearing you?

Has there ever been a season of silence between you and God—a season when you thought God was distant and it seemed as though He was not listening to you? Describe this time in your life.

How do you sense God hears, remembers, sees, or knows you right now? Ask yourself, What do I hear God saying to me?

Persevere as you go through the fire. Don't give up. —**Bianca**

 READ EXODUS 17:1–7. *Fill in your answers to these statements regarding the Israelites.*

- **GOD HEARD:**

- **GOD REMEMBERED:**

- GOD SAW:

- GOD KNEW:

How can you identify with the Israelites in this story?

How has God's silence affected you in the past? Or how has God heard you?

- RELATIONALLY:

- SPIRITUALLY:

- PHYSICALLY:

- EMOTIONALLY:

What blessings came out of your seasons of silence and the times when God heard you?

This is the confidence we have in approaching God: that if we ask anything according to his will, he hears us. —1 John 5:14

HEBREW HISTORY

UNDERSTANDING THE ANCIENT TEXT

HEARS:
Hebrew word is shamaʻ*; to be aware of; to listen to*

LISTEN:
Hebrew word is shamaʻ*; to pay attention, to understand*

Hebrew letters for God Hears:

אלהים שמע

Individual Prayer—Conversation with God

Since today's session is on listening and hearing, let your words be few. Use this time to craft one or two sentences—force yourself to be succinct—and ask God to prepare you for the next activity. In the silence, let Him speak to you.

Individual Activity (10 minutes)

Take a few moments to practice JOURNALING today. Write down words, thoughts, or pictures of whatever comes to mind when you think about God HEARING you. There are no right or wrong answers. This is a stream-of-conscious exercise. Just capture whatever thoughts, desires, frustrations, pictures, or prayers come to mind. Grammar rules do not apply—perfectionism is on pause. What do you sense God saying to you or showing you about how He HEARS you?

Use this space to write words, thoughts, or verses that come to mind. Be mindful of God's presence with you as you engage in this activity.

*Let the redeemed of the L*ORD *tell their story. … they cried out to the L*ORD *in their trouble, and he delivered them from their distress.*[9] —**The Psalmist**

Extra Credit (5 minutes)

We touched on the fact that God hears us during session one, but I want to dig a little deeper if you have the extra time today. Throughout the Israelites' 400 years of slavery in Egypt and their forty years of wandering in the wilderness, God heard their cries. Even when they thought He was silent and uninterested, God heard them. *So what is it like for you to wait to hear from God during a season of silence?*

Take a few moments to look up these verses and write down a few thoughts. *What does Scripture say about how God hears us?*

2 CHRONICLES 7:14–15

PSALM 46:10

PSALM 145:18–19

God's chosen people were mistreated, abused, and undervalued from the womb to the tomb. From the depths of their souls, they cried out to God, and He heard them.[10] —**Bianca**

DAY THREE
GOD REMEMBERS

Remembered and Reminded

The Israelites lived in an oral-written culture. This means stories were passed down from one generation to the next in spoken word until written word was more widespread and writing tools were more easily accessible.

The Old Testament book of Deuteronomy is a beautiful narrative of three sermons given by Moses to the Israelites. In this passage of Scripture, Moses remembered and reminded the Israelites of all that God had done for them in the desert. He essentially reminded the Israelites to remember the way God remembered them. (Are you with me?)

Many scholars believe the most significant section of this ancient text is Deuteronomy 6:4–6, known in ancient Hebrew as the SHAMA or SHEMA:

> *Hear, O Israel: The L*ORD *our God, the L*ORD *is one. Love the L*ORD *your God with all your heart and with all your soul and with all your strength. These commandments that I give you today are to be on your hearts.*

Jesus restated the SHAMA in Mark 12:28–31:

> One of the teachers of the law came and heard them debating. Noticing that Jesus had given them a good answer, he asked him, "Of all the commandments, which is the most important?" "The most important one," answered Jesus, "is this: 'Hear, O Israel: The Lord our God, the Lord is one. Love the Lord your God with all your heart and with all your soul and with all your mind and with all your strength.' The second is this: 'Love your neighbor as yourself.' There is no commandment greater than these."

Otherwise known as THE GREATEST COMMANDMENT.

Personal Study (15 minutes)

READ GENESIS 15:12-21. God foretold the slavery and deliverance of the Israelites. And then God remembered them. Think about a time when God remembered you. Where were you? What made you realize that God had remembered you?

How did God remember you?

Describe a time in your life when you thought you were forgotten by the people around you. What made you feel this way?

What is it like to be remembered by the people around you? How does it make you feel?

Are there situations or relationships in your life where you might be projecting your feelings on God? Where you feel forgotten by the people around you, so you feel forgotten by God?

What does God hear, remember, see, or know about you right now? What do you hear God saying to you?

 READ DEUTERONOMY 6. Fill in your answers to these statements regarding the Israelites.

- **GOD HEARD:**

- **GOD REMEMBERED:**

- **GOD SAW:**

- **GOD KNEW:**

How can you identify with the Israelites in this story?

The LORD remembers us and will bless us: He will bless his people Israel ... he will bless those who fear the LORD—small and great alike. —**Psalm 115:12–13**

How has God remembered you?

- RELATIONALLY:

- SPIRITUALLY:

- PHYSICALLY:

- EMOTIONALLY:

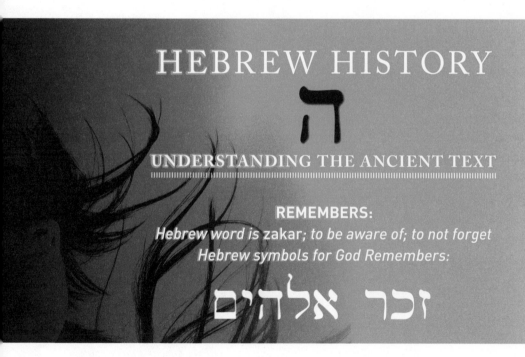

HEBREW HISTORY

ה

UNDERSTANDING THE ANCIENT TEXT

REMEMBERS:
Hebrew word is zakar; to be aware of; to not forget
Hebrew symbols for God Remembers:

אלהים זכר

Individual Prayer—Conversation with God

Use your own words to ask God to show you where you've felt forgotten in life—by Him or by the people around you. Ask God for forgiveness for the times you've projected your hurt from others onto Him. And thank Him for remembering you in so many different ways.

Individual Activity (10 minutes)

I love to journal. Most people think it's geeky, but I own my nerdiness and love the idea of chronicling God's fingerprint from the past to the present. I have journals from high school where I would take a Scripture and write it out repeatedly and then pray it out loud like I was speaking it to God to ensure He would hear me. My journals are personal reflections of how God has been present even in the silence.

Take a few moments to practice REFLECTION today. Find a quiet spot to reflect on the way God has remembered you. How has God remembered you in past or current moments of failure, insecurity, financial stress, relational struggle, pain, sorrow, and confusion? Write down whatever comes to mind.

And then, find something, perhaps a small object, that reminds you of a time when God remembered you. For me it's a journal, but for you it could be a rock, a colored leaf, a pressed flower, a picture, a piece of jewelry, or something decorative in your office or house. Whatever it is, put it in a place where you will see it often and be reminded, *"This was one of the many times when God REMEMBERED me."*

This is what the LORD, the God of Israel, says: "Write in a book all the words I have spoken to you."[11] *—God*

God wants you to walk in freedom and fullness instead of wandering and complaining.
—**Bianca**

Extra Credit (5 minutes)

We touched on the fact that God remembers us during session one, but I want to dig a little deeper if you have the extra time today. Throughout the Israelites' 400 years of slavery in Egypt and their forty years of wandering in the wilderness, God heard their cry. Even when they thought He was silent and uninterested, God heard them. *So what does it mean to know that God hears and remembers you? How does this change your everyday life?*

Take a few moments to look up these verses and write down a few thoughts. *What does Scripture say about how God remembers us?*

JOSHUA 1:3–5

PSALM 105:7–15

2 PETER 3:8–9

DAY FOUR

GOD SEES

Refined by Fire

I was teaching out of Malachi 3:3 and paused on this phrase: *"He will sit as a refiner and purifier of silver ..."*

I grew up in Los Angeles and never once heard of refined metal (or even knew what that meant), so the idea of a blacksmith or metalworking was so foreign to me. But the verse was referring to the nature and character of God, and I was obsessed with learning more. That week I called someone who knew someone who had some place that did something like metal work. It was far-fetched, but I decided to make a call and see what I could learn from a blacksmith. I didn't mention why I was researching this but merely made it sound like I was curious about the process of refining silver.

The silversmith explained that he held a piece of silver over the middle of the fire where the flames were the hottest and let it heat up. He did this because when the metal was at its hottest, all the impurities burned away.

As he said this, I thought about God holding me in a hottest spot of my own life and thought about Malachi 3:3 again, *"He will sit as a refiner and purifier of silver ..."* I asked the silversmith if he had to sit there in front of the fire the whole time. He said he not only had to sit there holding the silver but also that he had to keep his eyes on the silver the entire time it was in the fire. If the silver was left a moment too long in the flames, it would be destroyed.

I swallowed the lump forming in my throat and tried to keep from crying. In one sentence—in one moment—I felt like I was in the midst of the fire, and I knew that God saw me. I composed my voice and asked one last question: "How do you know when the silver is fully refined?"

He let out a small chuckle and confidently said, "Oh, that's easy. I know it's ready when I see my image in it."

If today you are feeling the heat of the fire, remember that God has His eye on you and will keep watching you until He sees His image in you.

Personal Study (15 minutes)

READ ISAIAH 40 (YES, THE WHOLE CHAPTER). Take note of all that God sees in this passage. What does God see, according to these verses?

When did you first realize that God could see you—see everything?

Sometimes we would rather hide our lives from God. Instead of willingly surrendering, we're forced to go through the "refiner's fire" to uncover what we're hiding. What are some things you might be trying to hide from God?

Where do you feel "unseen" in life right now? What makes you feel that way?

In session one, I said, "As I watched my life blazing, I was left with two choices— walk away from the flames or walk into them." When have you had to make a similar decision?

READ GENESIS 17:15–22. Think about what this chapter tells us about Abraham and Sarah's relationship with God. What do you think Sarah was feeling prior to God's message for her? How would Sarah answer these statements about God?

- **GOD HEARD:**

- **GOD REMEMBERED:**

- **GOD SAW:**

- **GOD KNEW:**

How has God used "refining fire" to change, redirect, or transform your life in the following ways?

- **RELATIONALLY:**

- **SPIRITUALLY:**

- **PHYSICALLY:**

- **EMOTIONALLY:**

Search me, God, and know my heart; test me and know my anxious thoughts. See if there is any offensive way in me, and lead me in the way everlasting.—**Psalm 139:23–24**

HEBREW HISTORY

UNDERSTANDING THE ANCIENT TEXT

SEES:
Hebrew word is ra'ah; to notice or become aware of

Hebrew letters for God Sees:

ראה אלהים

Individual Prayer—Conversation with God

Use your own words to ask God to show you how He SEES you. Ask God how He's refining your life with fire—holy fire. Where do you need a new perspective on life? Ask God for the courage to walk through the flames of life. And thank God that He not only sees you as you walk through the fire—but also that He is with you in the fire.

Individual Activity (10 minutes)

Take a few moments to practice PAYING ATTENTION today. Light a candle, build a fire in the fireplace or outdoor fire pit, and take a few moments to sit and pay attention. What do you SEE? What happens to the candle and the wick, or the wood? What do you see in those flames? How does the fire feel? Draw a picture or use words to describe your experience. Just as you are able to see through the flames of your fire, God sees through the flames of fire in your life. May you feel His presence in the warmth of the flames and fire and know you are seen.

Use this space to write words, thoughts, or verses that come to mind. Be mindful of God's presence with you as you engage in this activity.

Extra Credit (5 minutes)

We touched on the fact that God sees us during session one, but I want to dig a little deeper if you have the extra time today. God sees everything. He saw it all with the Israelites—their crying out and their complaining, their obedience and their disobedience ... you name it and God saw it. *So, what does it mean to you to know that God sees you in every aspect, in every area of life? How does this change your everyday life?*

Take a few moments to look up these verses and write down a few thoughts. *What does Scripture say about how God sees us?*

GENESIS 16:7–15 (THE STORY OF HAGAR)

MATTHEW 6:28–30

HEBREWS 4:13

God chose the Israelites because of themselves, not in spite of themselves. God intimately knew their pain, sorrow, and confusion. Even when we fall short, God STILL chooses us.
—Bianca

DAY FIVE
GOD KNOWS

Oh Yes, He Does!

God KNOWS. God knows who we are and what we're all about. God knows our passions, our desires, our cries, our pain, and our longings for purpose. God knows the visible and the hidden parts of our lives. God knows the real and the fake—*or, as I like to say, God knows the Rolex from the Folex (Fake + Rolex = Folex).* God knows our joy and our shame. God knows all of our successes. God knows all of our past, present, and future failures. AND GOD LOVES US ANYWAY.

Yes, my story of singleness has a happy crescendo into marriage and instant motherhood with two wonderful stepkids. But it's not perfect. Everything I learned in my desert season was put to test almost immediately in my new life. I went from being a single, debt-free, indie-movie-watching, world-traveling woman to an instant mom of two, driving a four-door car, living in an apartment, in a new city on a budget.[13] But God KNEW what I was stepping into and had prepared me in the desert seasons. I was ready for what I was about to step into, and He KNEW it.

I have indeed seen the misery of my people ... and I am concerned about their suffering.[12]
—**God**

In the same way ...

GOD KNEW THE ISRAELITES WOULD COMPLAIN IN THE DESERT, YET HE RESCUED THEM ANYWAY.

GOD KNEW THE ISRAELITES WOULD WISH THEY WERE BACK IN SLAVERY, YET HE RESCUED THEM ANYWAY.

GOD KNEW THEY WOULD GRUMBLE IN HUNGER AND THIRST, YET HE RESCUED THEM ANYWAY.

GOD KNEW THE ISRAELITES WOULD WORSHIP A GOLDEN CALF WHILE MOSES WAS AWAY, YET HE RESCUED THEM ANYWAY.

And in the same way God knew the Israelites, *He knows us.* And He knows there is a thief who comes to keep us from Him; an enemy who comes to kill, steal, and destroy (see John 10:10). And God knows the way of eternal life through Jesus Christ. But we must be willing to accept Jesus and follow Him.

Personal Study (15 minutes)

READ PSALM 103:13–18. God knows you. He knows your exact thoughts, your weaknesses, and your actions. What words would you use to describe your relationship with God?

Now describe the special relationship you have with your best friend, a spouse, parent, mentor, or sibling. What does it mean to be KNOWN by them?

How did you get to know them? What did you do? What questions did you ask? How do you act when you're around them?

God knows your sins, failures, and shortcomings just like He knew the sins, failures, and shortcomings of the Israelites. —**Bianca**

 READ ISAIAH 43:1–4. *What else does God know that is relevant to the Israelites'
situation? Fill in your answers to these statements regarding the Israelites.*

- **GOD HEARD:**

- **GOD REMEMBERED:**

- **GOD SAW:**

- **GOD KNEW:**

What else does God know that is relevant to your current situation?

**How do you sense you are known by God in the following areas of your life? Use
descriptive words.**

- **RELATIONALLY:**

- **SPIRITUALLY:**

- **PHYSICALLY:**

- **EMOTIONALLY:**

HEBREW HISTORY

UNDERSTANDING THE ANCIENT TEXT

KNOWS:
Hebrew word is yada'; to have understanding of; to recognize

Hebrew letters for God Knows:

ידע אלהים

Individual Prayer—Conversation with God

Use your own words to ask God to reveal to you how He KNOWS you—how He sees you, how He hears you, and how He remembers you. He knows everything about you and still loves you! (Can I get an AMEN to that? Lord knows I am SO grateful for His love for me and all my shortcomings!) Thank God for His grace, mercy, and love in your life. And ask Him to show you how to make your loved ones feel known and how to extend that same grace, mercy, and love to the people around you.

But now, this is what the LORD says—he who created you, Jacob; he who formed you, Israel: "Do not fear, for I have redeemed you; I have summoned you by name; you are mine." —Isaiah 43:1

Individual Activity (10 minutes)

Take a few moments to practice RECOLLECTION today. This might seem weird or foreign, but the act of remembering is biblical. The Israelites would gather around dinner tables and tell their history to their children and charge them to remember (see 1 Chronicles 16:15). They would even be reminded of their bad behavior while in the desert (see Deuteronomy 9:7–8).

Recollection is the act of remembering, so get into a comfortable position and settle down until you are free from distraction (as much as is possible). Think about this idea of being KNOWN by God. He knows your disappointments, your failures, your frustrations, your dreams, your passions, and your limits—and He loves you anyway. Recollect all the memories of God's faithfulness and trust that if He's gotten you **this** far, He will get you **that** far. Think of specific ways to remind yourself and others that they are known and loved by you AND by God.

You have searched me, LORD, and you know me.[14] —**King David**

Extra Credit (5 minutes)

We touched on the fact that God knows us during session one, but I want to dig a little deeper if you have the extra time today. And if you're anything like me, you may need to pause for a few seconds to wrap your mind around this truth: GOD KNOWS EVERYTHING. *So, what does it mean to you to know that God knows you inside and out? How does this change your everyday life?*

Take a few moments to look up these verses and write down a few thoughts. *What does Scripture say about how God knows us?*

DEUTERONOMY 2:7

1 SAMUEL 1:26–28 (The Story Of Hannah and Samuel)

JOHN 10:14–16

Crying out is a humble reminder that we need God for every moment of everyday.
—Bianca

FLAME

לֶהָבָה

noun \'flām\

A state of burning brightly

SURRENDER

"For I know the plans I have for you," declares the Lord, *"plans to prosper you and not to harm you, plans to give you hope and a future."* **—Jeremiah 29:11**

INTRODUCTION: Surrender in Sheer Desperation

I love police chases. Don't ask me why, but I do. There's something so intriguing about watching a car trying to escape from the police while zooming down the freeway. I stare, completely captivated, and wait until the chase comes to a stop. My favorite part is when the person being trailed by authorities comes to a wall, a barrier, or runs out of gas. Without fail, the driver gets out of the car with his hands up in an act of surrender. But it wasn't his first option. The driver surrendered because he could no longer run away.

Have you ever experienced surrendering out of sheer desperation? In a divine chase, God was pursuing me, but I tried running away. I wanted freedom, but the more I ran, the less options I had. I share one of these moments in my book when I hit a proverbial wall and the only thing I could do was surrender. Let me recap that story for you.

It was Valentine's Day weekend. I was working part-time as a makeup artist for special events and was booked to do makeup for a wedding in the hometown of my ex-boyfriend. We had an on-again off-again relationship. Perhaps it was the fact that I had bought a new convertible BMW (that I couldn't afford), or the fact that I was just in a wedding mood, or the fact that I was near the city where we shared so many memories, but I couldn't shake the thought of him. So I picked up my cell phone while driving home and dialed his number.

While his phone rang, I daydreamed and thought that maybe it would work this time. He finally answered, and his deep voice sounded safe and known and usual. It was all the things I longed for but didn't have. I wanted to talk to someone who would hear me. He was happy. I could hear it in his voice. Everything inside of me wanted to believe that the happiness I heard coming through the phone was because I had called him.

"I'm getting married," he exclaimed.

The air escaped my lungs and my head felt faint. I was driving eighty-five miles per hour on the freeway and had to pull over.

"Oh, greaaaaaat. How greaaaaat." It was said in the way my Southern college friends had taught me when you really are trying hard to be nice, but you don't mean it, with wide eyes, a large smile, and all those extra syllables. "Isn't this greaaaaaat. How greaaaaat is that?" I tried to understand how this had happened. Just two months earlier he asked me to take him back.

Eventually we hung up … and then I lost it. White-knuckled, red-faced, and tasting salty tears pouring down my cheeks, I lost it. "Where are You? Do You hear me? WHERE ARE YOU? Answer me, God! Answer me, please."[1]

In that moment of sheer desperation, I surrendered to God. I'm not sure I knew then, but stopping the car on the side of the freeway felt like the chase was over. I had nowhere left to go. I had exhausted every avenue of my self-imposed change and fallen miserably short. Through I didn't get out of my car and lift my hands in surrender, I think this was preparing me to allow God to take control and transform me into the woman He knew I was.

VIDEO TEACHING: Surrender (24 minutes)

Take a few minutes to play the video teaching for session two. As you watch, feel free to take notes or record any thoughts that stand out to you. Use the following concepts and questions to guide your group conversation.

Can you relate to my story on "controlling" my honeymoon experience or the story on hoarding? What do you hold on to out of fear? (Don't make me feel like I'm the only one!)

{RECAP}: DTR (Define the Relationship) = **GOD + THE ISRAELITES.**
Name a few things I share about God's relationship with the Israelites.

GOD:

GOD:

GOD:

GOD:

Letting go is a sign of maturity.—**Bianca**

God called Samuel in the middle of the night. *God called to Moses* in the middle of a burning bush. *Just like God beckoned Samuel and Moses, how is He beckoning you to step toward Him?*

Four questions Moses asked God:

1. WHO _____ ?

(Exodus 3:11–12)

GOD'S RESPONSE:

2. THEN WHAT _____ ?

(Exodus 3:13–14)

GOD'S RESPONSE:

Lay down your fear and see how God resurrects it to life!—**Bianca**

3. WHAT IF _____ ?

(Exodus 4:1–5)

GOD'S RESPONSE:

4. WHAT IF _____ ?

(Exodus 4:10–16)

GOD'S RESPONSE:

What is God asking you to surrender?

Where God has you is where God wants you.—**Bianca**

*Now Moses was tending the flock of Jethro his father-in-law, the priest of Midian, and he led the flock to the far side of the wilderness and came to Horeb, the mountain of God. There the angel of the L*ord *appeared to him in flames of fire from within a bush. Moses saw that though the bush was on fire it did not burn up.*—**Exodus 3:1–2**

GROUP DISCUSSION (21 minutes)

Okay friends, week two of KIR [Keeping It Real]! Our discussion will only go as far as we are willing to be honest. For us to have real change, we need to be real about where we are in our lives. Use these questions as a guide for group conversation:

{CONVERSATION STARTER}: **Share a brief story from your life when your dreams or plans didn't go as you had expected. What happened?**

What stands out to you this week about the story of Moses's doubt and insecurities? What did you hear?

What stands out to you about the way God responded to Moses's questions?

What do you think it means to SURRENDER? Share a few personal examples.

Just like Moses, we often ask, "Who am I?" or "Am I Enough?" In what areas of life are you asking these questions right now?

God used a burning bush to catch Moses's attention. What are the "burning bushes" in your life? Where is God trying to catch your attention? (This can be answered as individuals and as a group. Where is God trying to catch your attention as a group?)

How are you responding to those burning bushes? How are you responding to God's invitation to play with fire *in your own life?*

How does this teaching session change your perspective on life? Name at least one thing.

GROUP ACTIVITY (10 minutes)

Take a few moments in your group to once again practice honesty and vulnerability *together*. Ask each person to SHARE (out loud) one specific area she wants or needs to SURRENDER to God. Or, if that feels too personal, share what keeps her from surrendering to God. Write down each person's answers in the space provided below, and then be mindful to pray for everyone in your group this week.

GROUP PRAYER—CONVERSATION WITH GOD (5 minutes)

Prayer is personal, and I would never require it to be forced, repetitive, or scripted. If you want to pray out loud your own unique conversation with God, go for it, homegirl! But if you need help forming language to communicate to God, I've included this prayer for you here.

> *God, we thank You for this group and for this session. Thank You that You hear us, You remember us, You see us, and You know us. Please help us stop questioning and second-guessing You when You call out to us. Thank You for grabbing our attention in big and small ways, especially in those desert moments of life. We believe You are the same God who called out to Moses from the burning bush and invited him into the courageous act of freeing the Israelites from slavery in Egypt. God, we believe in Your power to RESCUE and LEAD us as we respond to Your personal invitation to play with fire. Thank You that You call out to us, and give us the courage to surrender to You. Please help us to encourage each other as a group over these next few weeks. AMEN.*

THANK YOU once again for being honest and vulnerable as individuals and as a group. God wants you to step into the fire with Him instead of playing it safe on the sidelines. All you have to say is, "Here I am, God." And now you have a few friends who are willing to step into the fire with you. So let's jump in together!

XO,

DAY ONE
LETTING GO

Painful Surrender

I'll never forget the day we found out my mom had brain cancer. I remember every detail of that day—the smell of my dorm room, the sound of students chattering on the walkway below, the feeling of my woven rug clenched tightly between my fingers, the taste of my hot tears streaming down my face as I lay on the floor. Everything. The moments are seared into my memory.

The salty tears stung my eyelids. I never saw this coming. None of us did. I was confused by how a good God would allow bad things to happen to good people. But more than confused, I was angry. Our family had sacrificed everything for the gospel and building the church worldwide.

And then I remembered the Israelites. From womb to tomb they were mistreated, abused, and undervalued. From the depths of their souls, they cried out to God. And He heard them. He understood their pain and remembered His promise to them.

In that moment of painful surrender, balled up on the floor, I cried out to God from the depths of my soul. With a ragged whisper, I begged Him to cover my mother and heal her like only He could.

I sat up in the midst of the chaos, confused, yet covered by God. I stood to my feet, trembling in fear, and asked Jesus to protect my mother. There was no thunder or lightning, but my soul heard a voice soft and was soothed. The words whispered to me, "Will you trust Me? Will you have faith that I am good even if it is bad?"[3]

God was asking me to SURRENDER—to let go and trust that He would take care of my mom and, in doing so, take care of me too.

Personal Study (15 minutes)

 READ EXODUS 3:1–6. Think about this moment in the life of Moses. How can you identify with Moses—his fears, his insecurities, his second-guessing that it was God calling out to him in the fire? Name a few specifics.

Describe a time in your life when God was trying to grab your attention and yet you "turned your face away" in fear. What was the situation? Where were you?

How did you surrender to God in that moment?

Think about your current reality. What is God asking you to surrender to Him right now? What does surrender look like in those specific areas of your life?

*It's in our surrender that God uses the fire to refine us.—***Bianca**

READ EXODUS 4:1–5: Fill in your answers to these statements regarding Moses:

- **GOD HEARD:**

- **GOD REMEMBERED:**

- **GOD SAW:**

- **GOD KNEW:**

What does God know about your pain and your suffering right now?

Ask God to transform your perspective on suffering and surrendering and to help you courageously face your pain and your fears. Where are you asking God, "HELP ME LET GO!"?

- RELATIONALLY:

- SPIRITUALLY:

- PHYSICALLY:

- EMOTIONALLY:

And now the cry of the Israelites has reached me, and I have seen the way the Egyptians are oppressing them. So now, go. I am sending you to Pharaoh to bring my people the Israelites out of Egypt.—**Exodus 3:9–10**

HEBREW HISTORY

UNDERSTANDING THE ANCIENT TEXT

SURRENDER:
Hebrew word is yahab; *to give the control or use of something to someone else*

LET GO:
Hebrew word is shamat; *to release or let drop*

Hebrew letters for Surrender:

Individual Prayer—Conversation With God

You're probably by yourself again while doing your homework. So this is the perfect time to practice praying out loud! There is something so powerful about verbalizing aloud your need to God. Think about trying to ask for directions without using words. Wouldn't that be difficult? And though God knows our innermost thoughts, prayer enables us to realize our need for Him and to voice that need to Him. He *delights* in answering our prayers.

Use your own words to ask God to show you where He's calling out to you from the burning bush in your life. Where is He asking you to let go and surrender? And then thank Him for this season of life—no matter how hard.

Individual Activity (10 minutes)

Take a few moments to practice UNPLUGGING today. Sometimes constant access to live news feeds, social media updates, content downloads, and endless text messages only fuels the feeling of control in our lives. So take a break today, as much as possible, from the constant demands you experience with technology. Whatever you need to unplug from or let go of today in order to be fully present in your interactions—do it. By doing so, you are giving the gift of your presence to God, to yourself, and to the people around you. God cares about the way you prioritize your time and your interactions with the people around you.

As you unplug, think about how much time you spend "plugged in" every day. How could you surrender some of this time to God?

How can you mentally simplify and let go of things in your life by unplugging?

Extra Credit (5 minutes)

We touched on the "shift of surrender" (by letting go) during session two, but I want to dig a little deeper if you have the extra time today. Throughout God's invitation to Moses and the transformational desert journey of the Israelites, there were pivotal moments—or shifts—of surrender to God. Often, those moments came in the heat of crisis or in the pain of suffering. But every time there was a shift of surrender, there was also a promise of God. And, because of Jesus, the same holds true for our lives today—we experience a shift when we decide to let go and surrender to God. *So, what shift of surrender have you noticed in your life lately as a result of letting go?*

Take a few moments to look up these verses and write down the **questions** or **promises** that emerged as God's people experienced the shift of surrendering their lives to Him over and over again.

JOB 11:13–15

MARK 10:28–31

EPHESIANS 5:1–2

My comfort in suffering is this: Your promise preserves my life.
—Psalm 119:50

DAY TWO
WHO AM I?

MOSES

Moses's life was pretty crazy. He was born into slavery as an Israelite infant, hidden in a basket made by his own mom, and placed into the Nile River by his big sister in order to protect his life. He was pulled out of the Nile by the Egyptian royal family, raised in the palace by the princess, and given authority over the Egyptians and his very own people, the Israelites. He became a murderer, fled to the desert, married a young woman named Zipporah, and became a shepherd just like his father-in-law, Jethro. At that point, Moses was around eighty years old. He had spent the first forty years of his life in royalty and the next forty years in the desert in obscurity.

But God saw Moses on the backside of the desert. And when God called out to Moses from the burning bush, He had Moses right where He wanted him—all alone, stripped of the pomp and circumstance of Egyptian royalty, and smack dab in the middle of the desert wilderness. From the blazing fire, God commanded Moses to go back to Egypt and lead the Israelites out of slavery. That was insane! Of course, Moses responded to God with questions of insecurity, doubt, and fear. Wouldn't you do the same?! Moses said, "Who am I? When people ask who sent me, what do I tell them? What if they don't believe me? What if I can't find the words to say?"

The story gets even better. "What's in your hand?" God asked. Moses held out his staff. In those days, the staff represented identity, income, and influence. Moses was a shepherd and a farmer. The staff represented his identity—who he was and what he did. Moses's sheep represented his income, his savings account, and his retirement plan. And Moses had his own property. He had influence and authority in his community.

God commanded Moses to throw the staff onto the ground, and it became a snake! He said to Moses, "This is so the Israelites will believe the LORD, the God of their fathers—the God of Abraham, Isaac and Jacob—has appeared to you" (see Exodus 4:1–5). God basically said, "Look, Moses, I have this under control. I know what I'm doing. Are you willing to surrender and lay down what you already have so I can bring it to life?"

God wants to do the same for you. He sees you on the backside of your desert experiences. And where He has you is where He wants you. Trust me.

Personal Study (15 minutes)

 READ EXODUS 3:10–11. *Think about a time when you responded to God, just like Moses, saying, "WHO AM I?" What was God inviting you into or asking you to do?*

What doubts, fears, or insecurities were you feeling in that moment? Why did you question God's invitation?

Moses's staff represented his influence, income, and identity. What are signs or symbols of influence, income, and identity today?

Think about your current reality. Where are you asking, like Moses, "WHO AM I?" Or, "AM I ENOUGH for this situation or opportunity?"

I love that the image of FIRE in the Bible always reveals the presence of GOD.—**Bianca**

 READ EXODUS 3:11–12. *Fill in your answers to these statements regarding God's response to Moses. How did God respond to Moses in the following ways throughout this story?*

- **GOD HEARD:**

- **GOD REMEMBERED:**

- GOD SAW:

- GOD KNEW:

What does this response say about how God viewed Moses?

Think about God's current invitation to you. How would your life change in the following areas if you responded to God's "big ask" with a loud YES?

- RELATIONALLY:

- SPIRITUALLY:

- PHYSICALLY:

- EMOTIONALLY:

What next steps do you need to take to surrender to God's invitation to you?

God also said to Moses, "I am the LORD. I appeared to Abraham, to Isaac and to Jacob as God Almighty, but by my name the LORD I did not make myself fully known to them."—**Exodus 6:2–3**

HEBREW HISTORY

UNDERSTANDING THE ANCIENT TEXT

THE LORD:
Hebrew word is Yahweh; *the proper name of the God of Israel*

Hebrew letters for Yawheh:

Individual Prayer—Conversation With God

Today's session is about questioning God in the midst of surrender by asking, "WHO AM I?" Use this time to actually ask that question directly to God in prayer.

Individual Activity (10 minutes)

Take a few moments to practice the spiritual discipline of EXAMEN today. This discipline, which derives from the Latin word for *examination*, encourages you to have a deeper sense of awareness regarding God's voice and His direction in your life. Spend a few quiet moments with God right now. Ask Him to make you aware of His activity in your life today as you think and pray through these questions:

What was the most life-giving moment of your day?

When did you have a deep sense of connection with someone today?

What drained you?

When were you least connected to your surroundings?

What is God saying to you in the midst of your doubts, fears, insecurities, and questions right now?

Be still and let God respond to you. Then write down what you sensed God saying to you during this time of Examen. Don't get discouraged if you experience silence. Sometimes God uses the people around us to answer the questions we pose directly to Him. So go about your day and be mindful of God's presence and His activity in all of your interactions.

Use this space to write words, thoughts, or Bible verses that come to mind. Be mindful of God's presence with you as you engage in this activity.

For this reason, since the day we heard about you, we have not stopped praying for you. We continually ask God to fill you with the knowledge of his will through all the wisdom and understanding that the Spirit gives.[4] —**The Apostle Paul**

Extra Credit (5 minutes)

We touched on the "shift of surrender" (by letting go) during session two, but I want to dig a little deeper if you have the extra time today. Throughout God's interactions with Moses, and the transformational desert journey of the Israelites, there was always a pivotal moment—or shift—when Moses and the Israelites decided to let go and surrender to God.

Moses experienced a shift when he allowed God to transform him through surrender. But this shift only happened *after* he asked a few revealing questions.

Moses was afraid. The man who had heard God in a burning bush in the middle of the desert and experienced God's miraculous signs was AFRAID. He was full of doubt and insecurities. Yet God patiently answered Moses's questions. And not only did God answer the questions, but each time He also answered with a promise. *So, how is God responding to your questions of doubt and insecurity with His patience and promises today?*

Take a few moments to look up these verses and write down your answers to the question, *What does it look like to surrender to God?* Various responses emerged throughout the Bible as God's people asked Him over and over again about what it meant to surrender and follow Him.

JEREMIAH 10:23

LUKE 14:33

GALATIANS 2:20

I lift up my eyes to the mountains—where does my help come from? My help comes from the Lord, the Maker of heaven and earth.
—**Psalm 121:1–2**

WHAT AM I SUPPOSED TO SAY?

The Right Words

As an eleven-year-old girl growing up in the hood, I struggled to read or write when the rest of my peers had already mastered these skills. There were jaunts, jeers, unkind words, and laughter from my neighbors or Sunday school peers, all at my expense. There was some teasing because I couldn't read or write, and more teasing because I weighed more than any other fifth grader that year.

On more than one occasion, I just took it because I didn't know what else to say. I would go home and think of the BEST retorts, responses, and retaliations. But of course it'd be too late, and I would lie on the grass in my backyard dreaming of the day I would be able to know what to say.

It seemed like all the words were locked in a vault inside of me, and I had lost the key. Even today, years later, I sometimes feel so ill-equipped to respond to people. As I prepare for a presentation at work or create a Bible study, I have the looming fear that Moses had: *what am I supposed to say?*

I'm not Moses, and I don't have the luxury of talking to a burning bush. Buuuuuut ... I do have a God who **provides** where He **guides**! Just as God was with Moses as he spoke with Pharaoh, God is with me during my presentation at work or behind a pulpit teaching the Bible!

When I begin to doubt I have the qualifications needed to do what I do, I quietly hold on to the word God gave Mo in Exodus 3:14: "I AM has sent me to you."*

---

* Side note: I don't quote Exodus 3:14 out loud because people might think I'm CrAzY, but I have a quiet confidence that I AM has placed me exactly where He wants me.

Personal Study (15 minutes)

 READ EXODUS 3:13. Think about a time when you responded to God, just like Moses, saying, "WHAT AM I SUPPOSED TO SAY?" What was the situation? Where were you? Who was the audience?

What doubts, fears, or insecurities were you feeling in that moment? Why did you question God?

Where do you think those doubts, fears, or insecurities came from? When have you been at a loss for words in the past?

Think about your current reality. Where are you asking, like Moses, "WHAT AM I SUPPOSED TO SAY?"

 READ EXODUS 3:13–18. Fill in your answers to these statements regarding God's response to Moses and the Israelites.

- GOD HEARD:

- GOD REMEMBERED:

- GOD SAW:

- GOD KNEW:

Think about a recent opportunity God gave you to surrender to Him (or maybe one He's giving you right now) by speaking up in a particular group or situation. What if you simply said, "Yes, God, I'll speak up!" instead of questioning, "What will I say?" How might that opportunity or situation change for the better in the following ways?

• **RELATIONALLY:**

• **SPIRITUALLY:**

• **PHYSICALLY:**

• **EMOTIONALLY:**

God said to Moses, "I AM WHO I AM. This is what you are to say to the Israelites: 'I AM has sent me to you. —**Exodus 3:14**

HEBREW HISTORY

UNDERSTANDING THE ANCIENT TEXT

I AM:
Hebrew word is ehyeh; *existed, was, am, to be*

Hebrew letters for I AM:

Individual Prayer—Conversation With God

Today's session is about questioning God in the midst of surrender by asking, "WHAT AM I SUPPOSED TO SAY?" Use this time to actually ask that question to God in prayer.

Individual Activity (10 minutes)

Take a few moments to practice the spiritual discipline of DISCERNMENT today. This discipline encourages you to not only learn to recognize God's voice and movement in your life but also to take delight in the process. Spend a few quiet moments with God right now. Ask Him to make you aware of His activity in your life as you think and pray through these questions:

Where do you need to ask God for help?

How do you need to wait for God?

What are the desires that surface in your head and your heart today?

How is God calling out to you from a "burning bush" in the midst of your doubts, fears, insecurities, and questions right now?

Be still and let God respond to you in this moment. Write down what you sense God saying to you during this time. Don't get discouraged if you experience silence. As I said yesterday, sometimes God uses the people around us to answer the questions we pose directly to Him. So go about your day and be mindful of God's movement in your life and the opportunities He provides for you to ask questions and discern answers.

Use this space to write words, thoughts, or whatever comes to mind. Be mindful of God's presence with you as you engage in this activity.

Playing with fire is, yes, dangerous, but it's also powerful when harnessed for good. Play with fire and see how your life is transformed.—**Bianca**

Extra Credit (5 minutes)

We touched on the "shift of surrender" (by letting go) during session two, but I want to dig a little deeper if you have the extra time today. Throughout God's interactions with Moses and the transformational desert journey of the Israelites, there were always moments when Moses asked God, "What do I say?" I can't tell you how many times I've asked this question too. "God, what do You want me to say to these people?" or, "How should I respond to this situation?" So, where are you asking God these questions—what you should say and how you should respond?

Take a few moments to look up these verses and write down your answers to the question, *What should I say?* You will see that responses emerged throughout the Bible as God's people asked Him over and over again what to say in certain situations.

DEUTERONOMY 34:9

MATTHEW 10:18–20

1 JOHN 3:22

For we are God's handiwork, created in Christ Jesus to do good works, which God prepared in advance for us to do.—**Ephesians 2:10**

DAY FOUR
WHAT IF THEY DON'T BELIEVE ME?

DOUBT

Have you ever felt like Moses when he uttered, "What if they don't believe me?" Or worse, have you ever felt like you don't even believe yourself? I have. That's why I like Moses. He didn't have an intimating persona; he had a realistic view of his inadequacies. But what is even more exciting to me is that even in the midst of his doubt, God still chose to use him.

When I was invited to be part of the staff at A21, a global anti-human trafficking organization, I literally thought of all the reasons why I couldn't, shouldn't, and wouldn't take the job.

I'm too young.

    I'm not educated for this job.

        I just got married and need to focus on my family.

            I watch reality television and read novels. I can't do this job.

After all my excuses had run out, I was left to face the fact that if God called me, He would equip me. When we operate in areas out of our depths, it precludes us from saying, "Wow! I'm so awesome. I knew I was amazing enough to do this!" Instead, when we walk in the fullness of what God is calling us to do and His work is accomplished, we can't help but say, "Wow! *God* did this!"

Let me save you a lot of time, stress, and energy by telling you to get over yourself and remove all your doubt. Stop making excuses and trust the One who called you and equipped you. "What if they don't believe me?" Who cares! God does, and with that, you won't need anything else.

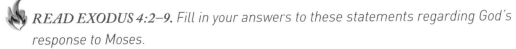

READ EXODUS 4:1. Think about a time when you said to God, just like Moses, "WHAT IF THEY DON'T BELIEVE ME?" What was the situation? Where were you? Who were the people you were afraid would not believe you?

What doubts, fears, or insecurities were you feeling in that moment? Why did you question God?

Where do you think those doubts, fears, or insecurities came from? Were they triggers from your past? Or relationships of mistrust and doubt? Or an unfamiliar group of people? Explain.

Think about your current reality. Where are you asking, like Moses, "WHAT IF THEY DON'T BELIEVE ME?"

Sometimes we ask this question when we share our faith with others, when we interact with our families (who know the best and worst about us), or when we have a word for someone. We'll talk more about having a word for someone in a later session.

READ EXODUS 4:2–9. Fill in your answers to these statements regarding God's response to Moses.

- **GOD HEARD:**

- **GOD REMEMBERED:**

- GOD SAW:

- GOD KNEW:

What was the significance of Moses's staff?

Think about a recent opportunity God gave you to surrender to Him (or maybe one He's giving you right now) by sharing something significant with the people in your life. What if you simply said, "Yes, God, I'll share it" instead of questioning, "What if they don't believe me"? How might that opportunity or situation change for the better in the following ways?

- RELATIONALLY:

- SPIRITUALLY:

- PHYSICALLY:

- EMOTIONALLY:

Do not let your hearts be troubled. You believe in God; believe also in me.—**John 14:1**

HEBREW HISTORY

UNDERSTANDING THE ANCIENT TEXT

BELIEVE:
Hebrew word is 'aman; to confirm, support

Hebrew letters for They Believe:

יַאֲמִינוּ

Individual Prayer—Conversation With God

Use your own words to ask God where you need COURAGE to do what He's asked you to do: to speak up, to step in, to shout out, to say something only you can say.

Individual Activity (10 minutes)

Did you know TRUTH-TELLING is actually considered a spiritual discipline? We spend enormous amounts of mental energy worrying about whether or not people will believe us, but that's not really the question we should be asking. The questions we should be asking are, *How can I be obedient to God? How can I respond to God's requests with obedience?* Walking in obedience often means that we are extra mindful to tell the truth. Sometimes telling the truth in certain situations seems a little dangerous, like *playing with fire*. But God is with you in those moments, just as He was with Moses! Take a few moments to think about this: *How, when, or where is God inviting you to tell the truth?*

Journal your answer to this question. Use this space to write words, thoughts, or Bible verses that come to mind. Be mindful of God's presence with you as you engage in this activity.

What, then, shall we say in response to these things? If God is for us, who can be against us?[5] —The Apostle Paul

Extra Credit (5 minutes)

We touched on the "shift of surrender" (by letting go) during session two, but I want to dig a little deeper if you have the extra time today. Throughout God's interactions with Moses and the transformational desert journey of the Israelites, there was always a pivotal moment of surrender followed by God's promises. But the story doesn't end there. Moses and the Israelites still had a choice as to whether or not to believe God. *So, how are you choosing to believe God's promises today? Is it hard to believe God's promises? Why or why not?*

Take a few moments to look up these verses and write down your answers to the question, *What does God say about our lives when we surrender and walk in obedience with Him?*

ZEPHANIAH 3:17

ISAIAH 1:18–20

MARK 10:28–31

> *But [the Lord] said to me, "My grace is sufficient for you, for my power is made perfect in weakness." Therefore I will boast all the more gladly about my weaknesses, so that Christ's power may rest on me.*
> —2 Corinthians 12:9

DAY FIVE
WHAT IF I CAN'T SAY THE WORDS?

SAY WHAT?

Have you been in a super awkward situation where you feel like you can't speak? Or, worse, you just can't get the words out? I have! But in those moments you can rely on God, who is always ready to fill your mouth when He asks you to speak. I remember one time specifically that changed my life ...

The auditorium was full, with almost a thousand youth pastors and youth volunteers. It was an annual youth workers conference, and church staff and volunteers from around the nation had gathered. We were told there would be a night of worship, and there we would be encouraged to pray for our youth ministries, church, and colaborers. I didn't know many people ... but the organizer of the conference was a longtime friend and encouraged me to attend, even if I came alone.

Acknowledging our weaknesses and expressing humility before the living God is exactly what we need for transformation to occur.—**Bianca**

During the last night of the conference, my friend stated he wanted us to hear from God—to trust God to move in our hearts and lives. During our time of worship, I sat down for a moment and closed my eyes to pray. And when I settled into this prayer, I saw a word appear in my mind.

I sensed I needed to do or say something about this word, but it was embarrassing. (You'll have to read the book to find out what it was—it may be a little too "risqué" to place in a women's Bible study guide!) I immediately went to shaming myself for not focusing on our time of worship. Then I remembered what my dear friend had said: "God will reveal and bring clarity when He is speaking to you."

I battled in my mind. *God, I can't say THAT! How do I know this is from you? If you're telling me something, prove it! What am I supposed to do with this?*

My friend opened the microphone for people to share Scriptures, words of encouragement, or anything else stirring in their hearts, and then he exited the stage. No one moved as the band continued playing. I can't use any other word to explain what I was feeling in that moment but *compelled*. I was compelled to stand up, walk through the crowded row of seats, and share what God told me.

As I made my way to the microphone in the front of the auditorium, God gently confirmed to me that I COULD say those words.[6]

READ EXODUS 4:10. Think about a time when you responded to God, just like Moses, "WHAT IF I CAN'T SAY THE WORDS?"—and then God confirmed His word to you. What was the situation? Where were you? What words were you supposed to say or share?

What doubts, fears, or insecurities were you feeling in that moment? What made you think you couldn't say the words?

How did God confirm His word to you in that moment?

Think about your current reality. Where are you asking, like Moses, "WHAT IF I CAN'T SAY THE WORDS? Help me, God!"

Sometimes we ask this question when we are on the verge of something big, even in the seemingly small things—a big breakthrough, a new understanding, a change in direction, or a shift in surrender—so pay attention to what else is going on around you when you feel this way. God might be up to something bigger than you realize!

 READ EXODUS 4:10–17. Fill in your answers to these statements regarding God's response to Moses.

- **GOD HEARD:**

- **GOD REMEMBERED:**

- **GOD SAW:**

- **GOD KNEW:**

Why did God get angry with Moses?

Think about a recent opportunity God gave you to share a few words, and yet the words didn't immediately flow and you needed some help. How did He rescue you by providing additional voices to speak into that situation? How did that situation change for the better in the following ways because God provided help?

- RELATIONALLY:

- SPIRITUALLY:

- PHYSICALLY:

- EMOTIONALLY:

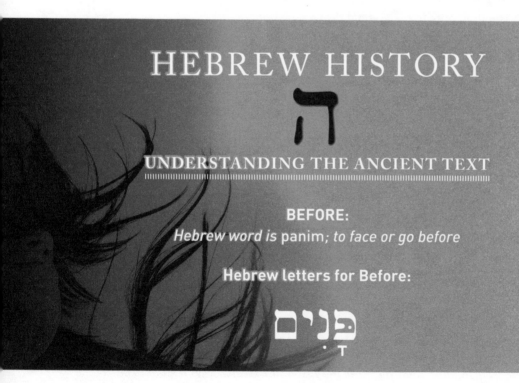

HEBREW HISTORY

ה

UNDERSTANDING THE ANCIENT TEXT

BEFORE:
Hebrew word is panim; *to face or go before*

Hebrew letters for Before:

פָּנִים

Individual Prayer—Conversation With God

Use your own words to ask God for help as you SURRENDER to Him. Ask Him how He wants you to share the words He's given you, and ask Him if there are other people you can invite into this process. Who else around you could speak into your situation? Who else around you is God inviting to *play with fire*?

Individual Activity (10 minutes)

Take a few moments today to reflect on the word JUSTICE. Did you know justice is also a spiritual discipline? Maybe God's invitation to you as He calls out from the burning bush really isn't about you. Maybe it's about others. Maybe, like Moses and the Israelites, it's about *justice* for others—speaking up when you see injustices and fighting for the freedom of others. Maybe God is inviting you to *play with fire* because it means releasing captives (spiritually, emotionally, relationally, and physically). So, if freedom is on the line and people's lives are at risk, don't you think God will give you the words to say or the people to join you in your message? Take a few moments to think about these questions:

What are the injustices around you?

How, where, or when is God inviting you into finding justice?

Who else could join you in this "freedom fire"?

Journal your answer to these questions. Use this space to write words, thoughts, or sketches of whatever comes to mind. Be mindful of God's presence with you as you engage in this activity.

And then the opportunity came for me to not just be a Freedom Fighter, but to be a Freedom Writer.[7] —**Bianca**

Extra Credit (5 minutes)

We touched on the "shift of surrender" (by letting go) during session two, but I want to dig a little deeper if you have the extra time today. Moses was afraid. The man who heard God in a burning bush in the middle of the desert, and who experienced God's miraculous signs, was AFRAID. He cried out, "What if I can't say the words?" And God provided help. God rescued Moses from his doubt and insecurities by providing someone to speak for Moses: his brother, Aaron. *So, how is God responding and rescuing you with His patience and promises TODAY?*

Take a few moments to look up these verses and write down your answers to the question, *How does God rescue us as we surrender to Him?*

ISAIAH 45:2–3

PSALM 37:7–9

LUKE 4:18

And he did it, rescued us from certain doom. And he'll do it again, rescuing us as many times as we need rescuing.[8] —The Apostle Paul

EMBER

גַּחֶלֶת

noun \ˈem-bər\

A glowing fragment from a fire

GOD'S PROMISES

I will not forget you! See, I have engraved you on the palms of my hands.
—Isaiah 49:15–16

INTRODUCTION: Remebering God's Promises

My sweet mama always had a thoughtful approach to life. And when we were at our worst, she always gave us her best. Here's what I mean.

We knew poverty and the sting of not being socially accepted. But God always seemed to provide. One particular day, when the fridge was empty and the pantry bare, my mother pulled out a large piece of butcher paper and taped it to the kitchen door. On the top of the page, she wrote in thick, bold letters: **"PRAYER LIST."**

With earnest humility and brazen faith, she told us that we served a God who heard our prayers and answered them in His perfect time. She knew we served a God who promised to be faithful, promised to provide, and promised to take care of all of our needs. She gave us each a marker and told us to list what we needed:

- **GRANDPA'S SALVATION**
- **A CAR**
- **FOOD**
- **A BUILDING FOR CHURCH**
- **OUTFITS FOR EASTER (THIS WAS MINE, OBVIOUSLY!)**

As the list grew, we poured out our prayers for each need. We bowed our heads, closed our eyes, and asked God to provide for us like He provided for the children of Israel. As quintessential church kids, we knew God provided water, manna, quail, and daily provisions while the Israelites were in the desert. Why couldn't He do the same for us? He was a God who kept His promises.[1]

VIDEO TEACHING: God's Promises (25 minutes)

Take a few minutes to play the video teaching for session three. As you watch, feel free to take notes or record any thoughts that stand out to you. Use the following concepts and questions to guide your group conversation.

NOTES

{RECAP}: DTR (Define the Relationship) = GOD + THE ISRAELITES.
Name a few things I share about God's promises to the Israelites.

GOD PROMISED:

GOD PROMISED:

GOD PROMISED:

GOD PROMISED:

Sometimes in the fog of fear, we forget that God loves us.—**Bianca**

Two types of promises:

1. _____ PROMISES

DEFINITION:

EXAMPLES:

The children of Israel let their forgetfulness affect their faithfulness.—**Bianca**

2. _____ PROMISES

DEFINITION:

EXAMPLES:

God can do for us what He's done for the Israelites.—**Bianca**

How do you know if your promises are from God?

*I am the LORD, the God of all the peoples of the world.
Is anything too hard for me?*—**Jeremiah 32:27** NLT

GROUP DISCUSSION (20 minutes)

Okay friends, week three of KIR [Keeping It Real]! Our discussion will only go as far as we are willing to be honest. For us to have real change, we need to be real about where we are in our lives. Use these questions as a guide for group conversation:

{CONVERSATION STARTER}: **At some point, we all say, "I will never ..." and then end up doing the very thing we said we wouldn't do. What is your "never" story?**

What stands out to you this week about the promises of God? What did you hear?

What promises have you made to God?

What promises do you sense God has made specifically to you?

God will equip us if He's called us and empower us if He's led us.—Bianca

How have you experienced the heartache of a broken promise? Have you ever caused someone else to experience the heartache of a broken promise? Explain.

In the video we looked at three ways of knowing when God gives us a promise. How have you experienced these aspects?

How does this teaching session change your perspective on life? Name at least one thing.

> *BE CAREFUL … there is danger in misinterpreting the Word of God to get what you want. Don't use Scripture to justify your decisions.*—**Bianca**

GROUP ACTIVITY (10 minutes)

Am I the only one who feels slightly awkward sharing in small group settings? No? Okay, great. But let's be awkward together and learn how to grow in our honesty and vulnerability. Ask each person to SHARE (out loud) one specific promise she has heard, sensed, or felt from God. Write down each person's answer in the space provided below. And if there is time, ask each person about the distractions, doubts, and fears she faces as a result of her promise, and write those down too. Be mindful to pray for everyone in your group this week.

GROUP PRAYER—CONVERSATION WITH GOD (5 minutes)

There is power in prayer, and I firmly believe when we vocalize our thanksgiving and praise, God smiles with great joy. Like a friend, He loves when we speak openly with Him, and He's always excited to hear from us. Use this time to close out your gathering with prayer. If you need help with language, I'm including a prayer that I'm praying over you. Feel free to borrow it!

God, we thank You for this group and for this session. Thank You that You hear us, You remember us, You see us, and You know us. Please help us stop questioning and second-guessing You when You call out to us. Thank You for Your promises throughout the Scriptures—to the Israelites and to us. We ask that You encourage our hearts as we cling to those promises. We ask for discernment and understanding as we listen to Your words. And we ask

for freedom from distractions, doubts, and fears that come from the enemy.
God, we love You and we praise You. AMEN.

THANK YOU for another session of honesty and vulnerability as individuals and as a group. We took *a lot* of notes in this session—but don't worry! We will unpack them in our personal study sessions. Remember this: God wants you to step into the fire with Him instead of playing it safe on the sidelines. And He's promised to be with you every step of the way!

XO,

Let us hold unswervingly to the hope we profess, for he who promised is faithful. **—Hebrews 10:23**

DAY ONE
PROMISES IN THE MIDST OF PAIN

When people are in pain or grieving, the last thing they need is to be doled out a spoonful of religious syrup. Can I get an AMEN?! As my mother lay in bed ... sick with cancer ... I didn't need or want "magnet Christianity"—those sayings that fit perfectly on refrigerator magnets. I wanted honest hope.

One weekend I walked in on my sickly mother smiling politely and trying her best to sit up straight on the couch, even though she was clearly exhausted and in pain. One of our family friends—a pastor's wife—sat across from her and spoke incessantly. I approached, greeted her, and propped up pillows to provide comfort to my mother. "I was just telling your mom that I lost ten pounds and cycled to Huntington Beach this past weekend," said her friend. "You know, so she can get her mind off of being sick."

Are you kidding me? I thought. I felt the blood drain from my face and my lungs tighten. *Is she really talking about her great body and perfect health, or am I delusional?*

I stepped in to rescue my mom, which resulted in a quick exit by her "friend." HELLO. I let it all out with my mom. "How can she call herself your friend? That conversation was a train wreck. Did she really think she was helping?" My mom shushed me and stifled a laugh. Not only was I funny, but she also secretly agreed with me.

In her true fashion, my mom pulled me in, pulled out her Bible, and opened to the book of Psalms. Her frail hands rested on the page as she smiled and read aloud the words of David: *"The righteous will flourish like a palm tree, they will grow like a cedar of Lebanon"* (Psalm 92:12).

"Bianca," she said, "this doesn't make sense right now, but God spoke to me. In His word, He spoke to me and said I'm going to flourish like a palm tree. I'm going to be okay."[2]

Personal Study (15 minutes)

 READ EXODUS 3:8. Think about God's three promises to the Israelites. Put yourself in their shoes. What are you—as an Israelite—thinking or feeling about God's promises in this Exodus journey moment?

How can you identify with the Israelites in captivity—and God's promises to them? Which promise stands out to you most? Why?

Have you ever experienced some sort of expression of captivity? Maybe a work situation you couldn't get out of, a bad relationship, financial debt, a trip gone bad, or ridicule for your beliefs? How did God rescue you from that situation?

In Isaiah 49:16, God said, "I have engraved you on the palms of my hands." What does this passage mean to you? How is this promise true in your life today?

God's promises are what we hold on to in the midst of the fire of transformation.—Bianca

READ MARK 16:14–20. I've heard it said that we can make a correlation between the Israelites and the disciples. After Jesus' death, the disciples were distracted and struggling with doubt and fear. Fill in your answers to these statements regarding the promises Jesus made to His disciples before He ascended into heaven.

- **JESUS HEARD:**

- **JESUS REMEMBERED:**

- **JESUS SAW:**

- **JESUS KNEW:**

Put yourself in the disciples' shoes. How do you think they felt after this conversation with Jesus?

How does believing in God's promises change your outlook on life in the following areas?

- **RELATIONALLY:**

- **SPIRITUALLY:**

- **PHYSICALLY:**

- **EMOTIONALLY:**

So I have come down to rescue them from the hand of the Egyptians and to bring them up out of that land into a good and spacious land, a land flowing with milk and honey.—**Exodus 3:8**

HEBREW HISTORY

UNDERSTANDING THE ANCIENT TEXT

RESCUE:
Hebrew word is natsal; *to deliver, to free from confinement*

Hebrew letters for Rescue:

נצל

Individual Prayer—Conversation With God

You're probably by yourself again while doing your homework. So this is the perfect time to practice praying out loud! There is something so powerful about verbalizing aloud your need to God. Use your own words to THANK God for His promises to the Israelites. THANK Him for the example they are to us regarding His lovingkindness and faithful commitment to His people then and now. THANK Him that those promises hold true for us today because of the birth, life, death, and resurrection of Jesus.

Individual Activity (10 minutes)

Take a few moments to practice GRATITUDE today. Most of us are familiar with this idea of giving thanks, but let's really get to the heart of gratitude today. Take a few moments to think about *what fills you with gratitude.* Time with family, solitude with God, experiences and adventures, blessing someone or being blessed, successes or opportunities, worship music, conversation with friends? Whatever it is, be intentional about paying attention to or incorporating these things into your life today.

Also, take a few moments to journal your gratitude list, and tell God why you're grateful for that particular entry. Use this space to write words, thoughts, or sketches of whatever comes to mind. Be mindful of God's presence with you as you engage in this activity.

Extra Credit (5 minutes)

We touched on the promises of God during session three, but I want to dig a little deeper if you have the extra time today. Throughout God's invitation to Moses and the transformational desert journey of the Israelites, there were pivotal moments where God made promises to His people. Often, those promises came in response to the Israelites' crying out, and usually right before God asked them to do something BIG. He literally asked all two-million plus Israelites to cross the Red Sea and head into the barren desert wilderness, where He promised to protect them. He basically said to the Israelites, *"What's about to go down with the Egyptians is purposeful—so trust Me! It will bring glory to Me and show the Egyptians that I am the LORD"* (see Exodus 14). Think about your own life. *When did God ask you to do something BIG and at the same time made a promise to you?*

Take a few moments to look up these verses and write down the promises of God written in these Scriptures.

EXODUS 14 (YES, THE WHOLE CHAPTER—YOU WILL THANK ME)

ISAIAH 40:29

PROVERBS 1:33

DAY TWO
PROMISES TO US

The Promise of a Palm Tree

The palm tree is unlike any tree in that it breaks things that try to bind it. While other trees absorb wires or bands, the palm can break any bind around its trunk. As my mom believed she was going to flourish like a palm, I held on to the belief that nothing could bind the work of the Lord in her life. Nothing could tie or sink into her identity; no wire could pierce her confidence. She was going to flourish.

Very few trees can grow in the desert, and very few flourish in dry terrain. But the palm not only grows and flourishes; it produces fruit. The roots of a palm creep deep down into hot sands to find water below the dry surface. Other trees—and people—might become uprooted in desert terrain because there is little capacity to grow strong roots there. But as the prophet Jeremiah says, "Blessed is the one who trusts in the Lord, whose confidence is in him. They will be like a tree planted by the water that sends out its roots by the stream. It does not fear when heat comes; its leaves are always green. It has no worries in a year of drought and never fails to bear fruit" (Jeremiah 17:7–8).

Natural disasters wreak havoc on some of the strongest trees. From hardwoods to pines, many massive trees have been uprooted during storms while palm trees remain. No matter what raging wind life would bring, my mother would stand like a palm. She would bend but not break. She would flourish.

As my mom's roots grew deeper during her season of sickness, I knew I had to grow roots of my own. I needed to come through my season of fire growing in my faith, my roots stretching deep into the hope of God. I had to grow up. I had to grow roots.[4]

Personal Study (15 minutes)

REREAD EXODUS 3:8. Think about God's three promises to the Israelites. How can you identify with the Israelites in captivity? How are you asking God to rescue you?

From what situation or circumstance in life do you wish God would remove you?

What are you asking God to replace in your life? The Israelites wanted to replace their captivity with freedom—how about you?

Maybe you want to replace fear with trust, loneliness with acceptance, illness with health, broken relationships with love, doubt with understanding, or scarcity with generosity. Where are you crying out to God today? What promises from God are you seeking?

The LORD will fight for you; you need only to be still.[3] —**Moses**

READ HEBREWS 11 (aka the "Hall of Faith" of the Bible). *Fill in your answers to these statements regarding the stories of faith that stand out to you.*

- **GOD HEARD:**

- **GOD REMEMBERED:**

- **GOD SAW:**

- **GOD KNEW:**

You express your faith in God by your obedience to Him. In what area of life do you struggle with obedience to God?

What are some of the things you've accomplished in the following areas of life as a result of your faith in God's promises?

- **RELATIONALLY:**

- **SPIRITUALLY:**

- **PHYSICALLY:**

- **EMOTIONALLY:**

For all the promises of God in Him are Yes, and in Him Amen, to the glory of God through us. **—2 Corinthians 1:20** NKJV

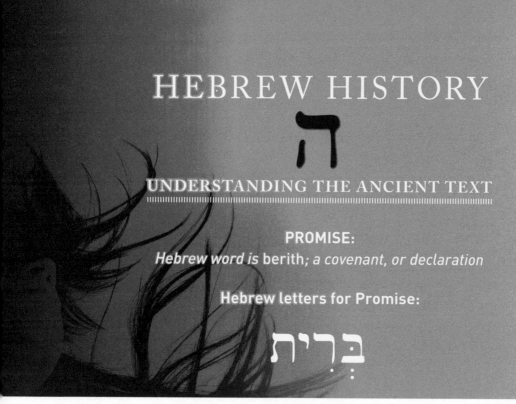

HEBREW HISTORY

UNDERSTANDING THE ANCIENT TEXT

PROMISE:
Hebrew word is berith; *a covenant, or declaration*

Hebrew letters for Promise:

בְּרִית

Individual Prayer—Conversation With God

Use your own words to acknowledge the promises God has made to you. Go ahead and pray out loud. What promises has God made to you recently or in the past? Speak them and tell God ways that you see Him being faithful to His promises. If you're unsure how to begin this prayer, go to the extra credit verses at the end of this session and pray the words straight from Scripture.

Individual Activity (10 minutes)

Take a few moments to practice the spiritual discipline of PRAYING SCRIPTURE today. This discipline encourages us to allow our prayer life to be shaped by words of Scripture. In doing so, we interact with God and listen to Him as we mediate on His words. Praying Scripture gives us the opportunity to adopt the prayers of the Old and New Testament authors as they cried out to God, received God's promises, questioned and reflected, and encouraged one another. So find your life verse, or a verse that speaks to you, and make it your own prayer to God in this moment. If you're unsure, use the extra credit verses again. Ask God to make you aware of His activity in your life as you pray and reflect on the words coming out of your mouth or filling up your mind.

Use this space to write words, thoughts, or verses of whatever comes to mind. Be mindful of God's presence with you as you engage in this activity.

The unfolding of your words gives light; it gives understanding to the simple.[5]
—The Psalmist

Extra Credit (5 minutes)

We touched on the promises of God during session three, but I want to dig a little deeper if you have the extra time today. Throughout God's invitation to Moses and the transformational desert journey of the Israelites, there were pivotal moments where God made promises to His people. Often, those promises came in response to the Israelites' crying out, and often right before God asked them to do something BIG. Think about your own life. *How have God's promises given you the courage to keep moving forward?*

Take a few moments to look up these verses and write down the **promises** of God written in these Scriptures.

ROMANS 10:9

PHILIPPIANS 4:19

2 PETER 1:3

DAY THREE
DISTRACTIONS

Forgetfulness

The Israelites, wandering in the wilderness, had seen God do the impossible. Just as I had seen and heard and witnessed the impossible, miraculous things God had done in my own life. But, oh, how quickly we forget.

As the Israelites forgot how God freed them from Egypt, I forgot the miracles God had continuously done in my life.

As the Israelites forgot about how God allowed them to walk across on dry ground through the Red Sea, I forgot about traveling in a car our family received as a benevolent gift.

As the Israelites forgot about how God had delivered manna to their doorstep daily, I had forgotten about the food provisions we had been given during my childhood.

When we forget what God HAS done, it makes us doubt what He CAN do. When we remember His promises, when we remember His goodness, when we remember His miracles, we can hold on to hope that He will rescue us in our time of need.

You know the way to the place where I am going.[6] —**Jesus**

Personal Study (15 minutes)

 READ EXODUS 15:22–27. *Think about the Israelites and the frustrations they encountered during their wilderness journey. What kind of frustrations did the Israelites face?*

How did God respond to this frustration? What caution or warning did God give to the distracted Israelites?

What distractions (doubt, fear, lies, past experiences, people, circumstances) keep you from remembering God's promises?

Has there ever been a time when you sensed God reminding you of His promises and cautioning you about your doubt, disbelief, or forgetfulness? What did you learn from that experience?

In your unfailing love you will lead the people you have redeemed.[7]
—Miriam and Moses

READ NUMBERS 13:16–33 AND NUMBERS 14:22–38. *Out of the twelve spies sent to explore the Promised Land, ten of them returned filled with doubt and fear about inheriting the territory. Only Joshua and Caleb had faith to walk into their promised land. Because of the Israelites' lack of faith, a whole generation died in the desert before the remaining Israelites were allowed to enter. Fill in your answers to these statements regarding the remaining Israelites in Numbers 14:22–38.*

- GOD HEARD:

- GOD REMEMBERED:

- GOD SAW:

- GOD KNEW:

How did God respond to Joshua and Caleb's faithfulness (see verse 24)?

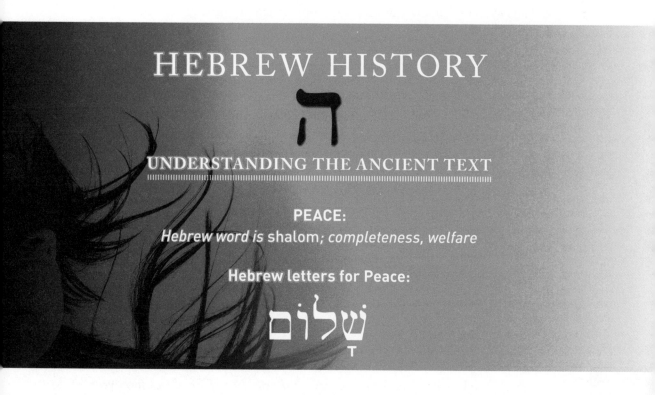

HEBREW HISTORY

ה

UNDERSTANDING THE ANCIENT TEXT

PEACE:
Hebrew word is shalom; *completeness, welfare*

Hebrew letters for Peace:

שָׁלוֹם

Individual Prayer—Conversation With God

Today's session is about recognizing distractions that keep us from remembering God's promises to us and for us—His followers—throughout history. Take a few moments today to acknowledge these distractions in prayer. And remember, there is also an enemy who longs to keep you distracted from your relationship with Jesus, so acknowledge him too. Express out loud your doubts, fears, distractions, and lies from the enemy that keep you from remembering God's faithful promises to you.

Individual Activity (10 minutes)

Take a few moments to practice the spiritual discipline of CONFESSION today. This discipline encourages you to regularly confess your distractions, your sins, and your forgetfulness to God. Write them down in the space provided below, or speak them out loud and invite God to shine His light into the darkness of those distractions and sins. Ask God to make you aware of what you need to confess to Him. *Where do you need to ask God for forgiveness?* After your own personal confession, invite a trusted friend, mentor, or family member into this process by asking them to help you see your blind spots. *Where do you need to ask them for forgiveness?*

Use this space to write words, thoughts, or sketches of whatever comes to mind. Be mindful of God's presence with you as you engage in this activity.

What should have been an eleven-day journey for the children of Israel took forty years of wandering in the wilderness because of doubt and fear.—**Bianca**

Extra Credit (5 minutes)

Throughout God's invitation to Moses and the transformational desert journey of the Israelites, there were pivotal moments where God made promises to His people. Often, those promises came in response to the Israelites' crying out, and often right before God asked them to do something BIG. Do you see the pattern?

God asks ➔ *God promises and reminds* ➔ *the Israelites respond* ➔ *the Israelites forget* ➔ *the Israelites complain and cry out* ➔ *REPEAT.*

Think about your own life. *Do you see a similar pattern in your relationship with God?* If so, ask God to help you break that cycle through confession.

Take a few moments to look up these verses and write down God's encouragement to you regarding distractions.

JOSHUA 1:8

1 CORINTHIANS 10:13

PHILIPPIANS 4:8

Be very strong; be careful to obey all that is written in the Book of the Law of Moses, without turning aside to the right or to the left.[8] —**Joshua**

DAY FOUR
DISCERNMENT

Is That Really You, God?

As a church kid, I grew up around a lot of Christians. As a pastor's kid, I knew the Bible stories and theology better than American history. As my parents' kid, I witnessed them hear from God in distinct ways, and I assumed I would grow up and learn to hear from God the same way. Whether it was communicating the Bible or praying for people, it was like they had a direct line to God, the way Commissioner Gordon had the red phone to Batman.

But when I became an adult (or at least looked like one), I still didn't "hear from God" like I thought I was supposed to. My law-loving, self-sufficient, legalistic side did all the right things from praying WITH people to being prayed over BY people to reading my Bible and studying exegetically. (You get me?) I wanted to know God's will for my life and hear from Him like I'd been told I could. I knew as a follower of Christ who was filled with the Spirit, I had the ability to hear from God. I just didn't know how.

After years of reading line upon line, verse upon verse, chapter upon chapter, and book by book of the Bible, I was discouraged and felt abandoned in my quest to hear from God. If His voice was a radio frequency, I was on a completely different bandwidth.[9]

Isn't that how life works sometimes? We pray, beat our chest, cry, scream, kick, and then without fanfare or dramatics, the Lord responds to us. When we reach the end of ourselves—when we surrender the burning up of all of our own promises—He speaks, and our life changes. This is the way it was with the Israelites too.[10]

Personal Study (15 minutes)

READ ISAIAH 61:1. The prophet Isaiah was certain of God's promises and purpose for his life. But how do we know when God has given us a promise, for real? In our video lesson, I shared the **DISCERNMENT PROCESS** I use when determining whether or not a word or promise is from God. Think about a recent promise you received from God—whether is was new to you or one you pulled from Scripture and sensed it was for you. What is that promise? Write it down.

How does that promise fit into this discernment process:

• How does it resonate with you?

• What does your community say about that promise?

• What is the fruit of you believing that promise? What comes out of your decision to respond to that promise?

So, what's next—is this really a promise for you from God? If not, can you use this same process for another promise God has for you?

Whenever I hear a promise from God from Scripture that resonates with me, I write it down, I believe it, I speak it, and I memorize it.—**Bianca**

READ HEBREWS 10:19–39. Fill in your answers to the following statements regarding the response of these Jewish Christians in the New Testament.

- **THEY HEARD:**

- **THEY REMEMBERED:**

- **THEY SAW:**

- **THEY KNEW:**

How do these promises speak to you today?

Think about each of these areas of your life. What promises do you sense God has for you in each area?

- **RELATIONALLY:**

- **SPIRITUALLY:**

- **PHYSICALLY:**

- **EMOTIONALLY:**

Let us hold unswervingly to the hope we process, for he who promised is faithful. —**Hebrews 10:23**

HEBREW HISTORY

UNDERSTANDING THE ANCIENT TEXT

FAITHFULNESS:
Hebrew word is ʾemun; to be faithful, trustworthy

Hebrew letters for Faithfulness:

אמן

Individual Prayer—Conversation With God

Use your own words to ask God to show you where you need to discern His promises to you. Ask God to reveal if you are misinterpreting His Word to get what you want, and ask Him to show you how to follow His true words.

Individual Activity (10 minutes)

We've already practiced the spiritual discipline of discernment in a previous session, so hopefully by now you understand the basics. Here's a spiritual discipline that goes hand in hand with discernment: ACCOUNTABILITY. Remember the second step in the discernment process? *What does your community say about that promise?* Well, here's a chance to put this into practice.

Practicing accountability requires you to invite a trusted friend, family member, or mentor to point you to Christ and help you live your life according to God's promises. This person should be someone who is capable of stepping into hard conversations, can ask challenging questions, and is willing to encourage, champion, and prayerfully support you. Take a few minutes to pray about this idea of accountability. Ask God who He wants you to reach out to as your accountability partner. If a couple of people come to mind, write their names down and continue to pray. Once you've made your decision, reach out to them.

Use this space to write words, thoughts, or verses that come to mind. Be mindful of God's presence with you as you engage in this activity.

Keep each other on your toes so sin doesn't slow down your reflexes.[11]
—**Author of Hebrews**

Extra Credit (5 minutes)

We touched on the promises of God during session three, but I want to dig a little deeper if you have the extra time today. We talked about the discernment process; however, we're not the only ones who have gone through this process. There are stories of people going through the discernment process in Scripture, including the ones in the following passages. *How does hearing these stories encourage you in your own faith journey?*

Take a few moments to look up these verses and write down the discernment decision mentioned in these Scriptures.

1 KINGS 3:10–15

2 CHRONICLES 2:12

PROVERBS 28:2

> *We also have the message of the prophets. This message can be trusted completely. You must pay attention to it. The message is like a light shining in a dark place. It will shine until the day Jesus comes. Then the Morning Star will rise in your hearts.* —**2 Peter 1:19** NIRV

DAY FIVE
WALKING FAITHFULLY

He Is Faithful

One night after work, while driving home to my parents' house, I found myself having a pity party. I was comparing and contrasting my life to everyone around me. But right in the middle of the world's best pity party, I found myself stopping my thoughts. I knew I was going down a dangerous road, and I didn't want to wallow in want or gripe in grief.

With everything in me wanting to fight the words, I uttered a prayer that sounded similar to the one Jesus prayed on a garden floor: "Not my will, but yours be done" (Luke 22:42). My eyes clouded with tears, but my thoughts were lucid. I was learning how to substitute my own will for the will of the Father.

I am your servant; give me discernment that I may understand your statutes.[12]
—The Psalmist

The last days of Jesus' life demonstrate the beauty of transformation.

He cried out to God.

    He surrendered His will.

        He knew the promise that His death would bring us life.

            He asked community to be with Him in the midst of trial.

                He listened even in the silence on the cross.

                    He resurrected from death to life.

I believed the power that resurrected Jesus Christ from the grip of death was alive in me. If Jesus promised me this same transformational power, I wanted it. I wanted ALL of it.[13]

Personal Study (15 minutes)

GENERAL PROMISES OF GOD. *During session three, I shared about two different kinds of promises: general promises and specific promises. Let's take a look at some of God's general promises throughout Scripture. What is a general promise? (Use your notes from the session three video teaching.)*

Read 1 John 1:19. **What is the general promise made in this passage?**

How does this promise impact you?

Read Philippians 4:7. **What is the general promise made in this passage?**

How does this promise impact you?

Whatever you have learned ... put it into practice. And the God of peace will be with you.[14] —The Apostle Paul

 SPECIFIC PROMISES OF GOD. Now let's take a look at some of God's specific promises throughout Scripture. What is a specific promise? (Use your notes from the session three video teaching.)

Read 1 Kings 9:5. *To whom is this specific promise made in this passage?*

How does this promise impact them?

Read Luke 2:35. *To whom is this specific promise made in this passage?*

How does this promise impact them?

Read Acts 13:47. *This is a throwback promise from Paul to Isaiah. Paul adopted what was a specific promise from Isaiah about the Messiah as a specific promise for himself. What is the promise made in this passage? How does this promise impact Paul?*

What are some of the specific promises you've made in life?

HEBREW HISTORY

UNDERSTANDING THE ANCIENT TEXT

MY PEOPLE:
Hebrew word is 'ammi; *people, folk*

Hebrew letters for My People:

Individual Prayer—Conversation With God

Use your own words to ask God to show you His general and specific promises for your life. Ask Him for direction in living out those promises. And THANK Him for the promises He's made to His people and to you specifically as His child.

Individual Activity (10 minutes)

Take a few moments today to think about the spiritual discipline of MEMORIZATION. The more you read God's promises from Scripture, the more you remember them. So why not dive in and actually memorize these promises? Memorization allows you to carry God's Word with you in your heart and your mind wherever you go. You can start with whatever promises God has already spoken to you, or you can start with some of the promises highlighted in the verses used throughout this session.

I will be with you.[15] —**God**

Wherever or however you decide to start—just START. Start with just one promise. Write it down on a Post-it note and place it where you will see it every day. Or set a reminder on your phone to check the verse on your Bible app at least once a day. And commit to adding a new promise each week. *As you think about and memorize God's promises, how do you sense God inviting you to play with fire?*

Use this space to write words, thoughts, or verses that come to mind. Be mindful of God's presence with you as you engage in this activity.

I have hidden your word in my heart that I might not sin against you.[16] —**The Psalmist**

Extra Credit (5 minutes)

Let's dig deeper! We talked about two different kinds of promises today: general and specific. But God is not the only one who gives promises. You've made promises, and promises have been made to you. *Name a few more promises you've recently made.*

Take a few moments to look up these verses and write down the promises of God written in these Scriptures.

EZEKIEL 36:26

PSALM 103:12

MICAH 7:9

And I will put my Spirit in you and move you to follow my decrees and be careful to keep my laws.[17] —**God**

I will say, "You are my people" ... and they will say, "You are my God."—**Hosea 2:23** NIRV

ASH

אֵפֶר

noun \'ash\

Solid matter left when something is completely burned; also symbolizes grief and repentance

COMMUNITY

Because of your great compassion you did not abandon them in the wilderness. By day the pillar of cloud did not fail to guide them on their path, nor the pillar of fire by night to shine on the way they were to take. **—Nehemiah 9:19**

INTRODUCTION: Better Together

I had an amazing group of friends whom I'd known for years. But distance, new professions, and changing seasons had pulled us in different directions, and the closeness we once experienced through proximity had left me feeling isolated and afraid of meeting new people. It was easy to come into church, sit in the back, and leave without ever connecting with anyone.

I liked being able to mask the pain and disappear when I felt vulnerability was required. I held to the lies that I was unlovable, unworthy, unwanted, or unable, and these lies kept me running after the idols I built for myself. Instead of exposing these idols to the community of faith, I hid in shame and embarrassment, like Adam hid from God in the Garden of Eden. But the safety of isolation was nothing more than a mirage; it wasn't what it seemed. Something needed to change; I needed to change.

The loss of relationships, my career advancement, and beating back my mother's well-meaning but emotionally unintelligent visitors was exhausting. I realized that if transformation was to occur and God's presence revealed, I needed to be in relationship with people. Open-fisted, I relinquished control and let new friends into the house I built in isolation—a house that was nothing more than ash, remnants of what once was.

I felt like a teenager asking someone on a date, except worse. I literally walked up to two girls I marginally knew—Jeanette and Diane—and nervously asked them if they would be my friends. Talk about awkward!

Over the course of months that rolled into years, we celebrated birthdays, successes, and full-on failures. After my flashpoint in the desert—after everything turned to ash—they became my oasis, my palm trees, the answer to my cry out to God ... and a reminder of His promises.[1]

VIDEO TEACHING: Community (25 minutes)

Take a few minutes to play the video teaching for session four. As you watch, feel free to take notes or record any thoughts that stand out to you. Use the following concepts and questions to guide your group conversation.

NOTES

The Israelite Community: What do we learn about the Israelites?

HEALTHY COMMUNITY:

UNHEALTHY COMMUNITY:

It's been said that truly great friends are hard to find, difficult to leave, and impossible to forget.—**Bianca**

{RECAP}: DTR (Define the Relationship) = **GOD + THE HEBREW HOMIES.**

Name a few things from the video teaching about the "Hebrew Homies" (Daniel, Shadrach, Meshach, and Abednego) from Daniel 3.

Five things we learn from the story of Shadrach, Meshach, and Abednego:

1. DECISIONS:

2. IDENTITY:

3. YOU:

4. REFINED:

5. GLORY:

SHADRACH Illuminated by sun god	**HANANIAH** Beloved by God
MESHACH Who is like Venus?	**MISHAEL** Who is like God?
ABEDNEGO Servant of Nebu	**AZARIAH** This is the Lord my God

GROUP DISCUSSION (20 minutes)

It's that time again! Yup, time to KIR. Our discussion will only go as far as we are willing to be honest. For us to have real change, we need to be real about where we are in our lives. Use these questions as a guide for group conversation:

{CONVERSATION STARTER}: **We all belong to some kind of club or social group. Share where you belong and why. (Note: If someone says "CatLoversAnonymous," just kick them out of the group. Stat.)**

Okay, back to our story in Daniel. What stands out to you this week? What did you hear or notice in this story?

In the beginning of this session, I asked, "Who is your community?" How would you answer that question?

There will be names people speak over you, but your number one name is CHILD OF GOD.—Bianca

Based on your own personal experiences, how would you describe healthy community? Unhealthy community?

In the teaching, I talk about the trap we fall into when making decisions. We say, "I'll be happy when—" (fill in the blank). How would you finish this sentence?

What labels have you put on yourself or allowed others to put on you?

In those moments, how does your community remind you of the promises of God?

GROUP ACTIVITY (10 minutes)

Take a few moments in your group once again to practice honesty and vulnerability *together*. Ask each person to SHARE (out loud) one specific area in life where she needs encouragement—where she needs to be reminded of the promises of God. Write down each person's answers in the space provided below. And be mindful to pray for everyone in your group this week.

GROUP PRAYER—CONVERSATION WITH GOD
(5 minutes)

PRAYER TIME! If you want to pray your own unique conversation with God out loud, go for it! But if you need help forming language to communicate to God, I'm including this prayer for you here.

> *God, we thank You for this group and for this session. Thank You that You hear us, You remember us, You see us, and You know us. Please help us to remember Your promises and to always see You in the midst of the fire in our lives. Thank You for the way You refine us, shape us, mold us, and rename us. Thank You for the community of people You've placed in our lives. And thank You for this specific group of women and for the community You've given to us here in this place. Show us what it looks like to live together and love one another the way You intended. God, we love You and we praise You. AMEN.*

THANK YOU for another session of honesty and vulnerability as individuals and as a group. Even though we took a brief pause from the desert journey of the Israelites, I hope you can identify with this story from Daniel 3 and see how it connects to the story of the Israelites and your own story. Remember this: God wants you to step into the fire with HIM instead of playing it safe with the little idols or comforts in your life. And He's promised to be with you in the middle of that fire!

XO,

> *But there are some Jews whom you have set over the affairs of the province of Babylon—Shadrach, Meshach, and Abednego—who pay no attention to you, Your Majesty. They neither serve your gods nor worship the image of gold you have set up.* —**Daniel 3:12**

DAY ONE
DECISIONS

Bloody Knees

I've always been a fighter. No matter what's thrown my way, I never stop, never quit. In my mind, I'm like Maximus from *Gladiator* or Demi Moore in *G.I. Jane*. But the truth is, I'm more like Daniel Ruettiger from the movie *Rudy*, the fifth-string football player from Notre Dame who, despite the odds, worked really hard and played one game in 1974.

My junior year of high school, I was the captain of the track team, and our first track meet of the season was a district invitational. I don't know what possessed me, a 5-foot-2-inch Mexi-Rican with no "hops" (I was short and couldn't jump high), but in my naiveté I thought I could run hurdles. I got into my starting blocks. To the left of me was Franisha, and to the right of me was Aisha, African-American sisters with thighs the width and length of Roman columns. I remained tightly poised in my starting blocks until the gun went off.

At the sound, I sprinted out onto the track with force and fury. Clearing the first two hurdles and rounding the bend, I was distracted by what looked like a gazelle leaping over the hurdles next to me. I glanced to my left and saw Franisha pass me with ease. Distracted and panicked, I felt my cadence being thrown off. Out of rhythm, I couldn't generate the force I needed to clear the next hurdle. My back knee grazed the top, causing me to land with a wobble. I had to scramble to keep pace.

I approached the fourth hurdle without the confidence and velocity I needed. This time my back knee hit the hurdle, and I fell. Determined not to be disqualified, I leapt to my feet and sprinted to the next hurdle, only to fall over it once again. On to the sixth hurdle—I fell. And the seventh. And the eighth. And the ninth.

By the time I reached the tenth hurdle with bloody shins and bruised knees, I had to lift up my legs to get them over the hurdles. I limped across the finish line as tears ran down my cheeks. To this day, I'm pretty sure I hold the state record for the longest 300-meter hurdle race. But I never quit. I never gave up, because I had decided long before the race that I WOULD CROSS THAT FINISH LINE.[2]

Personal Study (15 minutes)

 READ DANIEL 3:4–12. *Think about Shadrach, Meshach, and Abednego. What was King Nebuchadnezzar's decree? How did Shadrach, Meshach, and Abednego respond to that decree?*

Put yourself in the shoes of these young men. What doubts, fears, or insecurities would you have experienced if you were them?

How can you identify with their situation? How have you experienced a similar kind of pressure?

When have you had to stand out against the crowd because of a decision you made?

Because we know who we are, we determine how to live.—**Bianca**

 READ DANIEL 3:13–15. *Whoa! King Nebbie (we're on a nickname basis here) just pulled a trump card with these guys, and that trump card was called THE BLAZING FURNACE. Now, keep your Hebrew sandals on for just a few more minutes and pretend you don't know the rest of the story. Think about this from their perspective. How*

does these young men's decision to not bow down to the king potentially affect them in the following ways?

- **RELATIONALLY:**

- **SPIRITUALLY:**

- **PHYSICALLY:**

- **EMOTIONALLY:**

Think about a situation or experience when you felt a similar pressure or when you stood out from the rest of the crowd because of a decision you made. How did God make Himself known to you in the following ways?

- **GOD HEARD:**

- **GOD REMEMBERED:**

- **GOD SAW:**

- **GOD KNEW:**

We do not need to defend ourselves before you in this matter. If we are thrown in the blazing furnace, the God whom we serve is able to deliver us. —**Daniel 3:16–17**

HEBREW HISTORY

UNDERSTANDING THE ANCIENT TEXT

SAVE:
Hebrew word is yasha`; *He will deliver*

Hebrew letters for Save as "He will deliver":

Individual Prayer—Conversation With God

Use your own words to THANK God for how He's been faithful to you in the past during times of pressure, difficult circumstances, or life-changing decisions. Name those times and tell God how much His presence meant to you in those moments. Ask God to give you wisdom as you face decisions today and in the weeks and months ahead.

Individual Activity (10 minutes)

Take a few moments to PRACTICE God's presence today. Practicing God's presence essentially means seeing every experience in your day as an invitation to be with God. If you've grown up in the church, you may think more concretely about "time with God" as quiet time, weekend church attendance, and maybe a small group or women's Bible study during the week. But God wants us to remember that He's *always* with us, even when we don't take notice.

In fact, Deuteronomy 30:14 states, *"The word is very near you; it is in your mouth and in your heart so you may obey it."* God is with you. He's with you as you wake up, as you get ready for the day, as you wash dishes or commute to work. He's with you ALL THE TIME.

Take a few moments to actually list your activities and events for today in the space provided below. Pause and ask God to help you remember His presence during these moments. Use this space to write words, thoughts, or verses that come to mind. Be mindful of God's presence with you as you engage in this activity.

Extra Credit (5 minutes)

We touched on the idea of community through the story of Shadrach, Meshach, and Abednego during session four, but I want to dig a little deeper if you have the extra time today. Throughout God's invitation to Moses and the Israelites, and to Daniel and his three courageous Hebrew friends, there were pivotal moments where these individuals had to make crucial decisions—decisions that changed the trajectory of their lives. Think about your own life. *When did God ask you to make a decision that changed the trajectory of your life?*

Take a few moments to look up these verses and write down what decisions stand out to you in these Scriptures.

PROVERBS 3:5–6

ROMANS 16:17–19

JAMES 1:5–6

DAY TWO
IDENTITY

I Forgot My Name

There are times we want bargains or an easy way out of hard situations. There are times when we want to be plucked from the desert or the impending furnace. It's normal. And sometimes worshiping a false god—even the gods of materialism, relationships, or health—seems like the easy way out. But just because there's an easy road doesn't mean it's the right option.

In my desert wilderness, I tried anesthetizing emotions and desires so I didn't have to feel pain anymore.

Chronic shopping? Yes.

Credit card debt? Absolutely.

Eating to numb the pain? Sure.

I suffered from "desert brain" and forgot the ways God had provided for me and my family. I forgot my God-given name: CHILD OF GOD.

The reward for conformity is that everyone will love you except for yourself.—**Bianca**

The story of Shadrach, Meshach, and Abednego took place thousands of years ago, but aren't we faced with similar decisions today? Do we bow to the little idols that exist in our everyday lives? Do we respond like the society around us when the pressure is on? Granted, most of us will never encounter a ninety-foot statue of gold we're expected to worship, but nevertheless there are ways we bend our knee to keep ourselves safe, to go unnoticed, to avoid the fire.

If I were around during the times of King Nebuchadnezzar, I fear my desire for safety and—oh, I don't know, LIVING—would have trumped my convictions. Just put yourself in their shoes (well, sandals). They had been trafficked from their homeland. Their parents were most likely dead. They had been thrown into a new culture, new language, and new religion. Would I have been able to withstand the pressures they must have felt? Yet they remembered who they were in God.

The moment we forget who we are, we find ourselves bowing down to little gods with no power to transform us.[3]

Personal Study (15 minutes)

READ DANIEL 3:16–18. Think about Shadrach, Meshach, and Abednego. What stands out to you about this passage?

How can you identify with the conversation between these young men and the king? When have you spoken with such courage?

Can you think of a time when you wished you would have spoken up like this? How were you affected as a result of not speaking up or not standing up for what you believed?

Let's face it—we all lose our way at times and start finding our identity in things or people other than God. Who are those people or what are some of those things in your life? (Trust me, you will feel SO MUCH BETTER if you just write it all down—get it all out.)

 READ ISAIAH 43:1–3. Let's go back to the Israelites for a few minutes. Here we see, once again, how God reminds the Israelites of His promises. Fill in your answers to these statements regarding the Israelites in this passage from Isaiah.

- **GOD HEARD:**

- **GOD REMEMBERED:**

- **GOD SAW:**

- **GOD KNEW:**

What stands out to you about this passage?

> *Do not fear, for I have redeemed you; I have summoned you by name; you are mine.*—Isaiah 43:1

How does believing these promises for yourself—as if God were speaking directly to you—change your current perspective in the following ways?

- **RELATIONALLY:**

- SPIRITUALLY:

- PHYSICALLY:

- EMOTIONALLY:

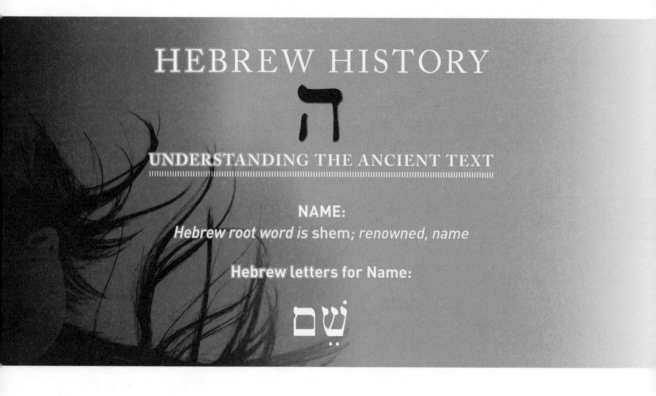

HEBREW HISTORY

UNDERSTANDING THE ANCIENT TEXT

NAME:
Hebrew root word is shem; *renowned, name*

Hebrew letters for Name:

שֵׁם

Individual Prayer—Conversation With God

Use your own words to thank God for WHO you are and to acknowledge WHOSE you are. You are a *child of God.* Go ahead and pray out loud. Ask God to help you truly believe Him, not just believe *in* Him. Thank Him for these stories from the Bible that demonstrate how you can have courage, strength, and confidence in His presence. Ask God to give you that same courage, strength, and confidence as you connect with members of your own community. And if you're still searching for this kind of community, ask God to help you find and gather these people in your life.

Individual Activity (10 minutes)

Take a few moments to practice the spiritual discipline of writing a RULE FOR LIFE. This is similar to the "one word" concept, in which you choose one word to represent your driving force for a year, except that rules for life can be words or phrases that remind you of your identity found in God.[4] Is there a certain promise verse that sticks out to you from this session or an earlier exercise? Is there a key phrase or word in that verse that reminds you of your identity in Jesus? If so, write it down and post it wherever you will regularly see it (and no, this is not your excuse from me to get a tattoo). If you have no idea where to start, look up 1 John 3:1 and begin there. This discipline will encourage you to be mindful of your true identity, found only in God and in Christ Jesus.

Use this space to write words, thoughts, or verses that come to mind. Be mindful of God's presence with you as you engage in this activity.

Don't put a period where God is not done with your story.—**Bianca**

Extra Credit (5 minutes)

We touched on the idea of community through the story of Shadrach, Meshach, and Abednego during session four, but I want to dig a little deeper if you have the extra time today. Throughout God's invitation to Moses and the Israelites, and to Daniel and his three courageous Hebrew friends, there were pivotal moments where these individuals had to make crucial decisions and stand firm in those decisions. They were able to stand firm in those decisions because of their convictions and beliefs—because they understood their identity in God. Think about your own life. *How have you stood firm in your faith when faced with a crucial decision regarding your identity?*

Take a few moments to look up these verses and write down what stands out to you about identity in these Scriptures.

See what great love the Father has lavished on us, that we should be called children of God! And that is what we are![5] —The Apostle John

Then Nebuchadnezzar was furious with Shadrach, Meshach, and Abednego and his attitude toward them changed. He ordered the furnace heated seven times hotter than usual and commanded some of the strongest soldiers in his army to tie up Shadrach, Meshach, and Abednego and throw them into the blazing furnace.—**Daniel 3:19–20**

IT'S NOT ABOUT ME

Are You Willing?

No matter where I lived, what I wore, or what color my skin was, God saw beyond that. Unfortunately, I didn't. When I started college, I decided to treat it as a time for reinvention. For me this meant shedding both weight and shame.

I ritually reminded myself that no one on campus knew I was once an illiterate child who shared a bedroom with my twin sister and snuck food into closets when no one was looking. No one I met knew I was poor or made fun of me because of where I lived or the color of my skin. No one in my dorm knew I'd witnessed demeaning prejudice against my father and his lingering accent. I buried in the recesses of my mind the shadow of the little girl who had hid under blankets. I ignored the memory of my first reinvention at the tender age of eleven and went on to pursue my own selfish attempt at transformation. I decided I would be perfect.[6]

But where in the Bible do we hear God say, "Thus sayeth the Lord—I mean, Me—I will only use perfect, polished, and pretty people"? Nowhere.

In the midst of the fire, I discovered that God cares less about ABILITY and more about AVAILABILITY. He used our Hebrew homies not because they were perfect (note how many other Hebrew exiles are *not* listed in Daniel) but because they realized it was not about them.

If you want to be used by God, stop focusing on what you don't have, what you aren't, or what you can't do. Are you willing? That's all that matters.

Personal Study (15 minutes)

READ DANIEL 3:19–23. Think about this scene between Shadrach, Meshach, Abednego, and King Nebuchadnezzar. What stands out to you in this passage?

Why do you think King Nebuchadnezzar's "attitude toward them changed" (verse 19) and he responded this way?

What does this passage bring to mind regarding your own personal experiences? When have you ever been this close to a real fire? Or when have you felt intense heat from a relational, spiritual, or emotional "fire" in your life?

How did God use that situation to bring awareness of Himself and glory to His name?

The LORD himself goes before you and will be with you; he will never leave you nor forsake you.[7] —Moses

 READ DANIEL 3:24–25. Whoa. There are few words to describe this scene. Can you IMAGINE? How would you respond to the following prompts in light of this passage?

- **GOD HEARD:**

- **GOD REMEMBERED:**

- **GOD SAW:**

- **GOD KNEW:**

In verse 25, the King said, "the fourth [man] looks like a son of the gods." What comes to mind when you think of this image of God? How would you describe God in the fire?

In one instant, King Nebuchadnezzar's world was turned upside down. The men he sent into the blazing fire were still alive ... and it appeared as though God was with them! What ramifications did this potentially have for King Nebuchadnezzar in the following areas of his life?

- RELATIONALLY:

- SPIRITUALLY:

- PHYSICALLY:

- EMOTIONALLY:

I am going to make you fruitful and increase your numbers. I will make you a community of peoples, and I will give this land as an everlasting possession to your descendants after you.—**Genesis 48:4**

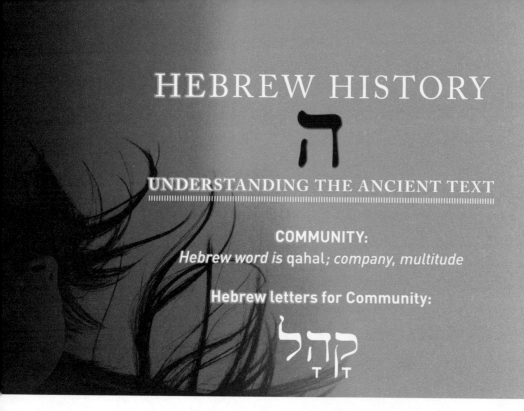

HEBREW HISTORY

ה

UNDERSTANDING THE ANCIENT TEXT

COMMUNITY:
Hebrew word is qahal; *company, multitude*

Hebrew letters for Community:

קהל

Individual Prayer—Conversation With God

Today's session is about recognizing that the fire in our lives is not always about us. Most often, God uses the fire in our lives to transform us in a way that brings honor and glory to Jesus—in a way that makes others notice God's refining work in our lives. Take a few moments in prayer today to acknowledge these transforming fires. Speak those moments out loud. Name them and thank God for how those fires transformed your life in specific ways. Thank Him for being with you in the midst of those fires.

Individual Activity (10 minutes)

Take a few moments to practice the spiritual discipline of COMMUNITY—the practice of journeying with one another and making particular relationships priority in our lives. God never intended for us to do life alone. He created us to be in community with one another—to encourage, support, and love one another, to bring out the best in one another, and to comfort each other as we go through transforming fires. All of this happens best in authentic community when we are honest and vulnerable enough to share our true selves with others and allow them to share their true selves with us. Reflect on these questions (feel free to revisit your teaching session notes if needed):

Who is this community for you?

How do you prioritize those relationships and make intentional efforts to journey together?

If you don't have this kind of community, whom could you invite into this journey with you—what kind of person?

Take a few minutes to sit still and ask God what He says about your future community. Use this space to write words, thoughts, or verses of whatever comes to mind. Be mindful of God's presence with you as you engage in this activity.

For where two or three gather in my name, there I am with them.[8] —**Jesus**

Extra Credit (5 minutes)

We touched on the idea of community during session four, but I want to dig a little deeper if you have the extra time today. Throughout God's invitation to Moses and the transformational desert journey of the Israelites, there were pivotal moments when God made promises to His people—but His people became distracted and forgot those promises. We looked at this pattern in the last session:

God asks ➔ *God promises and reminds* ➔ *the Israelites respond* ➔ *the Israelites forget* ➔ *the Israelites complain and cry out* ➔ *REPEAT.*

Think about your own life. *Do you see a similar pattern of distraction in your relationship with God?* If so, confess it to God and ask Him to help you break that cycle.

Take a few moments to look up these verses on community and write down what stands out to you.

ROMANS 12:16

HEBREWS 10:24–25

1 CORINTHIANS 1:10

DAY FOUR
REFINING MOMENTS

Panning for Gold

When I was ten years old, my mother took my siblings and me on a field trip to pan for gold. (Please don't judge us. We were weird.) There, a kooky mountain guide who wore canvas shorts, wool socks, and hiking boots explained to us the art of gold mining. He lifted up a massive piece of ore and said that hidden inside was something precious and valuable, but it was going to take patience to get it.

When you're a poor kid and someone tells you there's a possibility of possessing something lucrative, you sit down and listen! The hustler inside of me sized up the other kids in our tour group and did some mental calculations factoring in drive, tenacity, and stamina. I could outlast them all in the hunt for gold. In my mind, I was going to be RICH by the time I left for home.

But reality set in when our guide explained that the final step in acquiring gold was to break down the ore, to melt down the various rocks and fire up the gold until dross—otherwise known as junk—came to the surface. The fire would have to be white-hot, and would take continual stoking. The kids let out a combined sigh, because we knew it was way too much work for us and we didn't have the time to wait through the process. We weren't going to be taking any loot home.

Without missing a beat, our guide told us that was exactly the reaction most people had when they discovered how the process worked. Only dedicated and persevering people obtained the precious metal. "What survives in the fire," he said, "will determine what is truly valuable and real."

As we baked in the sun and scoured rocks, looking for gold-flecked fragments, we patiently tossed aside dirt clods, stones, and ore. We looked for precious metal amidst common elements. In hindsight, I see it. I might not have struck it rich that day, but I walked away with wisdom more valuable than gold.

What survives in the fire will determine what is truly valuable and real.[10]

Personal Study (15 minutes)

DANIEL 3:26–27. This. Is. Crazy. Not only were Shadrach, Meshach, and Abednego untouched by the fire, but the king also pulled them out of the fire, acknowledged God as the "Most High God," and CROWNED them. What stands out to you in this passage?

Keep in mind these young men were wrapped up and bound as this fire story plays out. Then the king sees them walking around in the flames! How have you felt wrapped up, trapped, and bound before a moment of transformation in your life?

What words would you use to describe King Nebuchadnezzar in this moment?

Sometimes God uses fire to transform our lives slowly—like roasting a marshmallow over the campfire. And sometimes God uses fire to transform our lives in an instant—bursting into flames like the Phoenix bird only to be made new again. How have you been transformed by fire—slowly or instantaneously—in your own life?

It's only when we're in the midst of fire that transformation occurs.—**Bianca**

READ DANIEL 6:1–23. A few years after the fiery furnace, and two kings later (another story for another time), we read the story of Daniel and the lions' den. Daniel was deceitfully set up in the same way as his friends and was forced to make a decision to stand firm in his faith. Answer the following prompts from the perspective of Daniel's story.

- GOD HEARD:

- GOD REMEMBERED:

- GOD SAW:

- GOD KNEW:

What stands out to you about Daniel's story?

What are some recent circumstances in the following areas of life where God has been faithful to you, yet AGAIN, in the midst some proverbial lions' den?

- RELATIONALLY:

- SPIRITUALLY:

- PHYSICALLY:

- EMOTIONALLY:

For You have tried us, O God; You have refined us as silver is refined.
—Psalm 66:10 NASB

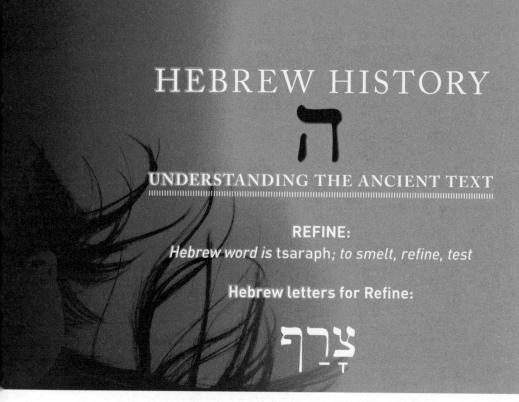

HEBREW HISTORY

ה

UNDERSTANDING THE ANCIENT TEXT

REFINE:
Hebrew word is tsaraph; *to smelt, refine, test*

Hebrew letters for Refine:

צָרַף

Individual Prayer—Conversation With God

Use your own words to thank God for the ways He has used fire to transform and refine you. Tell Him how your life is different as a result of those refining moments. Yes, He already knows, but there is something so powerful about voicing our gratitude out loud to Him and acknowledging His work in our lives. And if you're feeling fearful in this moment, as though you are wrapped up and bound—ready to be thrown in the fire—share those fears and anxieties with Him. Or, if you're in pain in the middle of the fire, cry out to God and tell Him how much you're hurting. He can handle all of your pain, hurt, sorrow, discomfort, and relief—ALL OF IT.

Individual Activity (10 minutes)

Today take a few moments to practice the spiritual discipline of REST. This practice honors God by acknowledging that we have human limitations. We are not God— He is God. HELLO. And rest is a gift from God. He created us with limits and the physical need to take a break, to sleep. So rest today—whatever it looks like, and whenever it works for you. And if you're on the go today, make the conscious decision to step into an unhurried pace. If you have time to sit or lie down—do it. If you have time to close your eyes—go ahead. And may you begin to create margin and rhythms of rest in your everyday life.

Use this space to write words or thoughts, or simply close your eyes. Be mindful of God's presence with you as you engage in this activity.

My soul finds rest in God.[11] —**King David**

Extra Credit (5 minutes)

We touched on the idea of community during session four, but I want to dig a little deeper if you have the extra time today. Throughout God's invitation to Moses and the Israelites, and to Daniel and his three courageous Hebrew friends, there were refining moments when these individuals had to walk through the fire in order to be transformed. Think about your own life. *What are you holding on to that keeps you from experiencing the transforming fire of God? What refining moments are you missing out on because you refuse to let go?*

Take a few moments to look up these verses and write down what stands out to you about these **refining moments**.

ISAIAH 48:10

MATTHEW 3:11

1 JOHN 1:5–7

Now to him who is able to do immeasurably more than all we ask or imagine, according to his power at work within us, to him be glory in the church and in Christ Jesus throughout all generations, for ever and ever! Amen.—**Ephesians 3:20–21**

DAY FIVE
GOD GETS THE GLORY

Through the Fire

In the story of Shadrach, Meshach, and Abednego, we see that the three young men confessed their faith *before entering the fire.* These boys stood up and defiantly punked the king, saying, "The God we serve is able to deliver us ... but even if he does not, we want you to know, Your Majesty, that we will not serve your gods or worship the image of gold you have set up" (Daniel 3:17–18). What confidence. What faith. What gall.

However, the young men's faith wouldn't be proved until they actually went *in the fire.* It wasn't until their faith was tested that it became real not only to them but to everyone else around them. When the boys were thrown into the furnace, King Nebuchadnezzar himself saw a fourth person in the flames. Biblical scholars debate who this was, but I believe it was a theophany. In the fire, the very presence of God was revealed to this band of brothers.

Fire will test the quality of each person's work.[12] —**The Apostle Paul**

Our deliverance isn't going to come from outside the furnace. The only way to get free is to go through the fire. It's in the fire that we are refined. It's in the fire that we are freed. The very thing that is supposed to kill us can free us and help us to enter the presence of God in ways we've never known.

I know it wasn't until I stood firmly on the promises of God that I was able to withstand my own furnace. And my community of friends? They made it easier. Nothing made sense and nothing seemed safe, but I knew I had to walk into what God was calling me into. It was as if He whispered, *Embrace the unknown and trust that transformation is awaiting you.*

As God said through the prophet Isaiah, "When you pass through the waters, I will be with you; and when you pass through the rivers, they will not sweep over you. When you walk through the fire, you will not be burned; the flames will not set you ablaze" (Isaiah 43:2).[13]

Personal Study (15 minutes)

 READ DANIEL 3:28–30. All glory to God! What stands out to you in this passage?

How does God get the glory in this story?

What happens to Shadrach, Meshach, and Abednego as a result of God getting the glory?

How might this moment change the trajectory of the lives of these young men, and the king? (Do a little dreaming here.)

How is God getting the glory in your own life—your own story—right now?

For no other God can save this way.[14] —King Nebuchadnezzar

 READ DANIEL 6:25–28. All glory to God, again. What stands out to you about the end of Daniel's "glory" story?

- **GOD HEARD:**

- **GOD REMEMBERED:**

- **GOD SAW:**

- **GOD KNEW:**

Now show me your glory.[15] —Moses

How is God getting the glory in your own life—your own story—in each of these areas?

- **RELATIONALLY:**

- **SPIRITUALLY:**

- **PHYSICALLY:**

- **EMOTIONALLY:**

How good and pleasant it is when God's people live together in unity!
—Psalm 133:1

HEBREW HISTORY

UNDERSTANDING THE ANCIENT TEXT

GLORY:
Hebrew word is kabod; *together, united*

Hebrew letters for Glory:

Individual Prayer—Conversation With God

Use your own words today to give God glory in your life. Or pray Scripture using the words of the apostle Paul in Ephesians 3:20–21: "Now to him who is able to do immeasurably more than all we ask or imagine, according to his power that is at work within us. To him be all glory ... Amen." Either way, take a few moments in prayer to acknowledge God's glory—for it is through Him, by Him, and for Him that we are transformed in the fire.

Individual Activity (10 minutes)

Take a few moments to think about the spiritual discipline of UNITY. Yes, God longs for us to have unity in community! And we practice unity by spending time with our community. This practice comes from the idea that we are one body of believers in Christ Jesus; therefore, we are called by God to live in unity, in love, and in peace with one another. And we are to be bridge-builders with those in the diverse communities around us. *How will you practice unity this week with your community? And with those outside your immediate community who bring diversity to your world?*

Use this space to write words, thoughts, or verses that come to mind. Be mindful of God's presence with you as you engage in this activity.

As far as it depends on you, live at peace with everyone.[16] —The Apostle Paul

Extra Credit (5 minutes)

We touched on community during session four, but I want to dig a little deeper if you have the extra time today. We talked about giving God all the glory, because we've been rescued by Him and transformed by His fire. Think about the last time you were rescued from something, someone, or a particular situation. *What part did the members of your community play in aiding you in that rescue?*

Take a few moments to write down the importance of unity in community found in these passages.

MATTHEW 18:20

HEBREWS 10:24–25

GALATIANS 6:1–2

It's not God, comma; it's not God, semi-colon; it's God, PERIOD.—Bianca

TRANSFORM

שׁבה

verb \tran(t)s-'form\

To change (something) completely

HOLY SPIRIT

*But the Advocate, the Holy Spirit, whom the Father will send in my name,
will teach you all things and will remind you of everything I have said to you.*
—John 14:26

INTRODUCTION: The Weekend Retreat

Who knew that one weekend could change my life? I didn't realize it then, but I can
see it now. Sitting behind the wheel of my car, the desert sun beat down on us as
Mom and I drove through empty lands. My mother glowed as she chatted about
how happy she was that hundreds of women's lives were forever impacted through
the church's annual women's retreat. With every ounce of her being, she believed
we'd progressed—in micro and macro ways—into a fresh understanding of who
God was and of His immense love for us.

Maybe she was right. I had heard, saw, and felt something going on in that
gathering of women. There was a smoldering ember that ignited the collective
faith, and this fresh faith spiritually awakened even the staunchest of doubters
(read: me). Although we didn't have a pillar of fire leading us through the desert
like the Israelites, in some way a fire had started in our hearts that led to revival.

The final day of the retreat, the prayer team had called my mom to the front of the
room. One of the leaders pushed her forward in her wheelchair, and the women
placed their hands on her body and began to pray. In a beautiful moment of
spontaneity, women from all over the auditorium stood to their feet, walked to the
front where my mother was seated, circled around her, and began to pray out loud.
The melodic cadence of their voices filled the room.

I watched as women cried out to God for a miracle. I don't remember what was said, but I remember what I felt: *hope.*

While I didn't feel a metamorphic shift or hear the audible voice of God, I knew my faith was awakening. There was something inside me that wanted change. The façade was crumbling, the veneer thinning—I needed a transformation. I not only wanted to hear from God again, but I also wanted to believe His promises. If He could make the old new, the dead alive again, and the crooked straight, I wanted to believe He could change and transform me into the person I was destined to be.

As my mom recounted the weekend on that desert drive, I nursed this prayer: *God, work in me.*[1]

VIDEO TEACHING: Holy Spirit (26 minutes)

Take a few minutes to play the video teaching for session five. As you watch, feel free to take notes or record any thoughts that stand out to you. Use the following concepts and questions to guide your group conversation.

NOTES

Define the **Promised Land** ...

FOR THE ISRAELITES:

FOR US:

Define the **Holy Spirit:**

{RECAP}: DTR (Define the Relationship) **= THE HOLY SPIRIT + PEOPLE.**
Name a few things I share about the Holy Spirit at work in the lives of these people in the Bible:

DAVID:

DEBORAH:

PETER:

PAUL:

Ancient Greek. *Write the definition of the following Greek words:*

PARA:

EN:

EPI:

GOD + JESUS + HOLY SPIRIT:

SUPERNATURAL:

NATURAL:

Holy Spirit Perspectives:

KNOW:

SEE:

FEEL:

HEAR:

EMPOWERED:

Very truly I tell you, whoever believes in me will do the works I have been doing, and they will do even greater things than these, because I am going to the Father.—**John 14:12**

GROUP DISCUSSION (19 minutes)

Okay friends, this is our LAST SESSION! I hope and pray that you have made it all the way to the end and that you have been honest not only with yourself but with others. For us to have real change, we need to keep being real about where we are in our lives. Use these questions as a guide for group conversation:

{CONVERSATION STARTER}: **What is an area of life you would say you are strong in? Physical strength? Emotional stability? Relational capacity?**

What was your understanding of the Holy Spirit prior to this teaching? (This is a judgment-free zone!)

What stands out to you about this week's teaching? What did you hear or notice?

What do you think of when you hear the words "Promised Land"? What does this look like for followers of Jesus today?

You don't know God is all you need until God is all you have.[2] —Corrie ten Boom

---

How would you describe your own personal Promised Land—the place where you sense God inviting you into His presence?

Which example can you identify with the most from the Old and New Testament people and their interactions with the Holy Spirit?

We see in the New Testament that Jesus' miracles were both supernatural and natural. What natural miracles has the Holy Spirit made you aware of and empowered you to do?

Categories might feel limiting, but we want to simplify. When it comes to experiencing the Holy Spirit, are you a knower, seer, hearer, or feeler? (It's okay if you don't know yet. Ask God to help show you!)

My Promised Land ... is being the presence and fullness of God.—**Bianca**

GROUP ACTIVITY (10 minutes)

Take a few moments in your group to once again practice honesty and vulnerability together. Ask each person to SHARE (out loud) one specific area in life where she wants to be empowered by the Holy Spirit—where she wants or needs to be MORE THAN ABLE. Write down each person's answer below. Be mindful to pray for everyone in your group this week.

GROUP PRAYER—CONVERSATION WITH GOD
(5 minutes)

This is our last time together for this study. My personal desire is that we will feel MORE THAN ABLE to pray and thank God for what He's done in our lives. Whether you are alone or in a group, I remind you that you are empowered and privileged to chat with God directly. Do you feel brave enough to pray out loud? I hope so. If you need help forming a prayer, I've listed one here for you.

God, we thank You for this group and for this session. Thank You that You hear us, You remember us, You see us, and You know us. And thank You for allowing us to experience the Holy Spirit as we know, see, hear and feel Your presence. Please help us to remember Your promises and see You in the midst of the fire in our lives. Thank You for the way You refine us, rename us, and transform us. Thank You for our time together as a community. Help us to encourage one another in the power of Your Holy Spirit as we move forward from this place. God, we thank You, we love You, and we praise You. AMEN.

THANK YOU for your honesty and vulnerability as individuals and as a group throughout this *Play with Fire* series. Remember this: God wants you to step into the fire with Him, and He's empowered you with the Holy Spirit so that you are MORE THAN ABLE to survive the transforming fire! Thank you for sharing this journey with me.

XO,

Speak, Lord, for your servant is listening.—1 Samuel 3:9

DAY ONE
THE SPIRIT SPEAKS

The Drive Home

Remember that retreat I told you about in this week's session? Well, as I drove home from that retreat with my mom, I nursed a growing notion of what *abundant life* was. The women's retreat had been held at a retreat center in the desert; we were in the desert both physically and metaphorically. My mother was undergoing chemo treatments at the time, and as I stared at her head—once full of thick, red hair—her swollen face, and her jaundiced eyes, I saw abundance. In her most fragile state, she believed in a God who was MORE THAN more than enough.

She was exhausted and drained, but she possessed more than enough love, more than enough joy, and more than enough hope. She had the abundant presence of a living God. Cancer had attacked her body but could not get to her soul. Her body was deteriorating, but her spirit was growing in strength. In spite of illness and pain, she had wanted to lead the retreat because nothing was going to stop her from creating an experience for women to learn about God and hear from God, even if it took her last breath. And she wasn't the only one with this mindset.

All weekend I had been with women who had real-life pain and real-life issues, but they gave from an internal reservoir that was more than enough. Cindy's son was a drug addict. Sylvia's husband was suffering from diabetes. Donna's mom was in the hospital. Mary's husband had passed away. And yet these women committed, year after year, to give from a depth carved out by pain but filled by God. The Holy Spirit filled what life had hollowed out.

The road, dusty and dry, stretched out in front of us as we continued our drive in the desert. I was leaving the retreat center physically and heading back home, but in a way, I was also heading back home in my heart. I longed to be in a place where God would speak to me. I never doubted He could; I just questioned if He *would*. The silence was natural, but the hope I began to feel in my chest was supernatural. I felt a resurrection coming. I felt a Phoenix rising from the desert ash.[3]

Personal Study (15 minutes)

 READ THE STORIES OF THESE BIBLE HEROES. Write down how these individuals experienced the power of the Holy Spirit in these stories.

DAVID (1 SAMUEL 16:1–13):

DEBORAH (JUDGES 4:4–23):

PETER (MATTHEW 6:18–20 AND MATTHEW 16:13–20):

PAUL (ACTS 9:1–19):

I want us to be women of the WORD.—**Bianca**

 THINK ABOUT IT. We can learn so much from these stories. Pick a story from the previous questions that speaks the most to you. How would you answer the following prompts based on that story?

- GOD HEARD:

- GOD REMEMBERED:

- GOD SAW:

- GOD KNEW:

How can you invite the presence of the Holy Spirit to be with you in the following ways today?

- RELATIONALLY:

- SPIRITUALLY:

- PHYSICALLY:

- EMOTIONALLY:

In what ways do you need the comfort or the power of the Holy Spirit's presence today?

He said, "Listen to my words: When there is a prophet among you, I, the Lord, reveal myself to them in visions, I speak to them in dreams."—**Numbers 12:6**

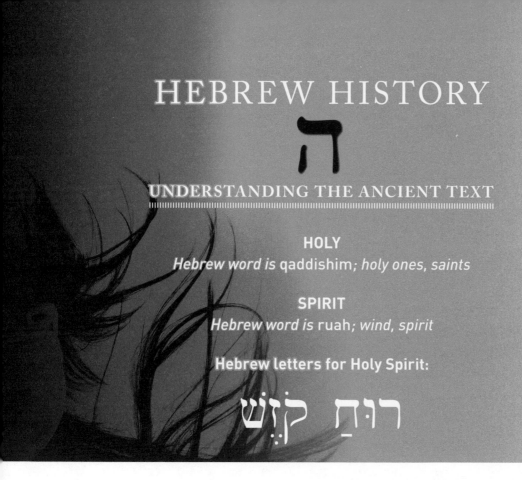

HEBREW HISTORY

ה

UNDERSTANDING THE ANCIENT TEXT

HOLY
Hebrew word is qaddishim; *holy ones, saints*

SPIRIT
Hebrew word is ruah; *wind, spirit*

Hebrew letters for Holy Spirit:

רוּחַ קֹדֶשׁ

Individual Prayer—Conversation With God

Use your own words to THANK God for times in the past when He's been with you through the comfort and power of the Holy Spirit. Name those times and tell God how much His presence meant to you in those moments. Ask God to give you wisdom as you discern the movement of His Spirit in your life today.

Individual Activity (10 minutes)

Take a few moments to practice INTERCESSORY PRAYER today. Intercessory prayer means handing over your worries, concerns, doubts, fears, and insecurities to God in prayer, and then joining God in prayer for the world around you. Ask Him to give you eyes to see what He sees as you consider these questions:

HOW DOES GOD SEE THE WORLD AROUND YOU?

WHO IS GOD CONCERNED FOR?

WHO IS GOD HURTING FOR OR LONGING FOR?

WHO IS GOD CELEBRATING?

Intercessory prayer means stepping out of your own prayer and entering into God's prayer. This might sound a little nebulous, but just try it. Ask God for help—He's with you in this very moment.

Use this space to write words, thoughts, or verses that come to mind. Be mindful of God's presence with you as you engage in this activity.

Through the prompting of the Holy Spirit, we have direct access to hear from God. We might not hear Him the way other people do, but we need to trust that God is speaking to us, and through us, by His Spirit.[4] —**Bianca**

Extra Credit (5 minutes)

We touched on the idea of the Holy Spirit during session five, but I want to dig a little deeper if you have the extra time today. We learn so much about the Holy Spirit when we read stories from the Bible and as we pay attention to the stories of the people around us—our community! *Who around you has a "Holy Spirit story" that has inspired you, impacted you, or encouraged you to be more aware of the Holy Spirit's presence in your life?*

Take a few moments to look up a few more verses of stories where the Holy Spirit spoke throughout the Bible. What were the visual signs of His presence, or what happened to reveal His presence?

1 SAMUEL 10:10

ACTS 1:8

ROMANS 8:26–27

Hope does not put us to shame, because God's love has been poured into our hearts through the Holy Spirit, who has been given to us. **—Romans 5:5**

DAY TWO
WITH GOD

Uncontrollable Flames

When I was in college, we used to gather on the upper lawn of the campus and build a massive bonfire during Homecoming weekend. When I say "massive," I'm not being dramatic (shocker?). Crates were stacked on a wooden foundation towering high in the air and lit ablaze while drunken college students screamed nonsense about our rival team and the upcoming football game. It was the liberal arts college version of Burning Man (minus the desert, hippies, and the fire marshal).

There were no fire extinguishers and no distinct boundaries to contain the flames. It was open and uncontrolled. It was beyond dangerous and ridiculously scary. For our whole lives, well-intentioned parents had told us not to play with fire. And now, while these same parents paid $45,000 a year for private educations, their children danced wildly around unruly flames.

I stood back and stared in awe, wonder, and reverential fear. Soon enough, though, I approached the flames myself, dancing dangerously in the warmth of the fire's glow. These flames, though powerful and scary, were also inexplicably beautiful.

Looking back, I knew the Holy Spirit intellectually, but I didn't know the Holy Spirit intimately. I stood back and watched flames from afar, but I needed to dance dangerously close and see the beauty of something uncontrolled. When I invited Jesus to be my personal Lord and Savior, I welcomed in the Holy Spirit to govern in my life. But looking back on the women's retreat, on the drive home, I see it. That was the moment I asked the power of the Holy Spirit to come upon me and empower me to do what God had called me to do. It was powerfully scary, but it was also beautiful.

Like the Israelites wandering in the desert, I wanted hope. Like the Israelites, I wanted my cry to be heard and my heart to be known. I wanted the prayers from the depths of my soul to be recognized and acknowledged. But what I needed was a FIRE. What I needed was surrender to the powerfully dangerous step of transformation.[5]

Personal Study (15 minutes)

UNDERSTANDING ANCIENT GREEK. *Okay, girls, as I like to say, it's time to "Greek Out." (I know, my homeschool humor is a little too much to handle.) Let's go back to the three main Greek words used in Scripture to describe the Holy Spirit. Read the following verses and write down what you hear regarding the Holy Spirit. Feel free to add anything else that stands out to you.*

JOHN 14:17: PARA, "ALONGSIDE, WITH"

JOHN 14:17: EN, "IN"

ACTS 2:4: EPI: "UPON"

And afterward, I will pour out my Spirit on all people.[6] —**God**

 READ ACTS 2:1–4. This is perhaps one of the most controversial passages of Scripture regarding the Holy Spirit in the New Testament because of the reference to speaking in tongues. However, let us not miss the most important point of this passage. Right in the middle of this story, the Holy Spirit moved from a promise to a Presence. Jesus promised the Holy Spirit would come, and He did. How would you answer the following prompts in light of this story?

- **GOD HEARD:**

- **GOD REMEMBERED:**

- **GOD SAW:**

- **GOD KNEW:**

The promise [of the Holy Spirit] is for you and your children and for all who are far off—for all whom the Lord our God will call. —**Acts 2:39**

Read the rest of Acts 2. *How does the Holy Spirit moving from a "promise to a presence" motivate, encourage, comfort, or challenge you in the following ways?*

- RELATIONALLY:

- SPIRITUALLY:

- PHYSICALLY:

- EMOTIONALLY:

HEBREW HISTORY

UNDERSTANDING THE ANCIENT TEXT

PROMISE:
Hebrew root word is neder; *meaning to vow, to promise*

Hebrew letters for Promise:

נֶדֶר

Individual Prayer—Conversation With God

Use your own words to thank God for the promise and the presence of the Holy Spirit in your life and in the collective lives of the community of believers. It is because of the Holy Spirit that God lives "in" and "alongside" and "upon" you.

Individual Activity (10 minutes)

If you were born in the '80s or '90s, you might remember *power walking*. Wristbands, ankle weights, and spandex were all the rage! But I've got something EVEN BETTER: *prayer walking*. Prayer walking is the idea of taking a walk and praying at the same time. If possible, be intentional about the place you pick, and choose a place that you are concerned about to walk around. Make sense? Are you concerned about your family? Then walk around your home! Are you concerned about something at work? Take a walk around the building! Concerned about something at school? Take a walk around the campus! Concerned about grammar usage? Use exclamation marks!

In doing so, you acknowledge that God is present with you in those places where you're walking. You acknowledge that He cares about that place and has a vision for the people in that place.

Use this space to write words, thoughts, or verses that come to mind after you take your walk. Be mindful of God's presence with you as you engage in this activity.

I urge, then, first of all, that petitions, prayers, intercession and thanksgiving be made for all people.[7] —**The Apostle Paul**

Extra Credit (5 minutes)

We touched on the idea of the Holy Spirit during session five, but I want to dig a little deeper if you have the extra time today. Scripture refers to the Holy Spirit as an intercessor—the "go between" for us. In fact, *intercession* can be defined as "prayer, petition, or entreaty in favor of another."[8] The Holy Spirit prays for and intercedes for us in our favor.

We have different gifts, according to the grace given to each of us.[9] —The Apostle Paul

Take a few moments to look up these verses and write down the ways you see the Holy Spirit acting as an Intercessor.

JUDGES 3:9–10

ROMANS 8:14–16

ROMANS 8:26–27

So since we find ourselves fashioned into all these excellently formed and marvelously functioning parts in Christ's body, let's just go ahead and be what we were made to be, without enviously or pridefully comparing ourselves with each other, or trying to be something we aren't.
—**Romans 12:6** MSG

DAY THREE
IN THE FIRE

Feeling the Heat

Throughout the Old and New Testaments, we find that God has responded by, appeared in the form of, and been likened to FIRE.

God was with Moses in a burning bush. God was with the Israelites in a pillar of fire as He led them out of slavery. God was with Shadrach, Meshach, and Abednego in the fiery furnace. God was with new believers as He transformed and empowered them with the fire of the Holy Spirit.

In every case, fire is seen as a symbol of God and His ability to radically change our lives.

Fire was alive and well in my life during the diagnosis of my mom's illness, my breakup with my ex-boyfriend, my college graduation, and my dreadful unemployment. Did this mean God was at work? Or did this mean that I was paying penance for something I had done or a mistake I had made?

In the firefighting community, there is a phrase that is used to express a critical moment in the beginning stage of a fire. This moment occurs when the temperature gets to a certain level where everything combustible in a room spontaneously bursts into flames, spreading the fire immediately and instantaneously. This is called the "flashpoint"—the point at which everything that can burn will burn.

In those days, the temperature of every area of my life had simultaneously reached a level of combustion. It started to feel like a scene from the movie *Backdraft* or *Ladder 49*. Fire seemed to be everywhere. Relational. Physical. Familial. Financial. Spiritual. There was heat on all fronts, and as I reached my flashpoint, everything I ever wanted burned down around me. As I watched a life blazing, I was left with a choice: walk away from the flames, or walk into them.[10]

You will be forced to make the same decision. And I pray you enter in boldly.

Personal Study (15 minutes)

 READ ABOUT THE MIRACLES OF JESUS. During session five, we talked about the supernatural and natural miracles of Jesus. Write down the supernatural miracles of Jesus found in these passages.

MATTHEW 8:23–27 (THE STORM):

LUKE 7:11–18 (THE WIDOW'S SON):

LUKE 8:43–48 (THE BLEEDING WOMAN):

JOHN 5:1-9 (THE BETHESDA MAN):

The Spirit of the living God is alive in us today.—**Bianca**

 READ MATTHEW 14:15–21. Respond to the following prompts in light of this passage.

- **JESUS HEARD:**

- **JESUS REMEMBERED:**

- JESUS SAW:

- JESUS KNEW:

Based on your understanding of Jesus, what kind of natural miracles did He perform?

As followers of Jesus, we use His life and His teachings as an example for our own lives. If this is true for you, how can you participate in the natural miracles of Jesus within the context of your everyday life in the following ways?

- RELATIONALLY:

- SPIRITUALLY:

- PHYSICALLY:

- EMOTIONALLY:

He led them out of Egypt and performed wonders and signs in Egypt, at the Red Sea and for forty years in the wilderness. —Acts 7:36

HEBREW HISTORY

UNDERSTANDING THE ANCIENT TEXT

SIGNS:
Hebrew word is 'owth; a sign, to tell

WONDERS:
Hebrew word is mophet; a wonder

Hebrew letters for Signs and Wonders :

אֹתֹת וּמוֹפְתִים

Individual Prayer—Conversation With God

Use your own words to ask God to show how you can be a part of the natural miracles around you. His invitation is always extended, but it's up to you to accept His invitation and move to join Him where He's already at work in your community. And ask God to give you faith to see the supernatural miracles He's performing around you. Thank Him for the work He's doing in and through you right now.

Individual Activity (10 minutes)

Take a few moments to practice the spiritual discipline of FASTING—the practice of letting go of your appetite for something or removing distraction in order to clearly see God. Please hear me out: *Fasting does NOT always mean abstaining from FOOD.* The last thing we need is a group of Bible study girls starving themselves "for the sake of Jesus." This is not the latest diet fad—this is an actual spiritual practice.

Now, some of you may sense you need to abstain from food in order to be more aware of God's presence in your life today. But for others, it may mean abstaining from social media, coffee, soda, your favorite reality TV show, that addictive game app, or lunch room conversation because it spirals out of control so easily. If you're unsure of what to fast from—ask God. If you're unsure what to pray about as you fast—ask God. Let's not make this too complicated. Take a few minutes to pause and ask God how He wants you to fast and what He wants you to prayerfully pay attention to during that fast.

Use this space to write words, thoughts, or verses that come to mind. Be mindful of God's presence with you as you engage in this activity.

She ... worshiped night and day, fasting and praying.[11] —The Physician Luke

Extra Credit (5 minutes)

We touched on the Holy Spirit during session five, but I want to dig a little deeper if you have the extra time today. Throughout Jesus's life, He performed signs and wonders, supernatural miracles and natural miracles. And when He ascended into heaven, the promise of the Holy Spirit became the presence of the Holy Spirit. *How does this knowledge shape the way you think about your own life? Do you see signs and wonders, supernatural and natural miracles, around you?*

Instead of looking at several miracles, I want you to focus on one. Read the passage listed below and take a few moments to really unpack this narrative. What stands out to you in this story? List all the fun details and dive into the meat of this man's miracle!

JOHN 9:1–38

Unless you people see signs and wonders ... you will never believe.[12] —Jesus

DAY FOUR
HOLY SPIRIT

Anointing

In the Old Testament, anointing was a beautiful, symbolic act of commission and recognition. According to biblical history, a ram's horn full of oil would be poured on the chosen king, priest, or prophet. The oil was poured on the head to give wisdom; over the ears so the person would hear from God; over the eyes so he or she would see what God sees; and over the hands so the person would do what God wanted to be done.

In Paul's second letter to the Corinthians, he reminded them (and us) to stand firm in Christ. He wrote, "It is God who makes both us and you stand firm in Christ. He anointed us, set his seal of ownership on us, and put his Spirit in our hearts as a deposit, guaranteeing what is to come" (1:21–22). WE are anointed! Not with a ram's horn full of oil, but with the Holy Spirit who comes upon (*epi*) us.

I know we might come from different denominational and church backgrounds, and we might understand the Holy Spirit within different paradigms. (I get it. I grew up in a conservative church where the Holy Spirit was discussed theologically, but it seemed scary and I didn't know why I should care.) But I want us to at least agree that we are **anointed** to do what God has called us to do, **sealed** with the ownership of Jesus Christ, and the Spirit is **within** us to do what we are called to do.

When we take a look at Scripture, we see ordinary people doing extraordinary things because they are filled with an *extraordinary* God. David was an anointed shepherd who went on to kill a lion, slay a giant, and win military battles. Deborah was a woman who, filled with the Spirit as a prophetess and judge, led God's people to victory. Peter was an uneducated fisherman who, filled with Spirit, gave one of the greatest apologetic defenses of the entire gospel (see Acts 3). And the apostle Paul was knowledgeable of God, but once filled with the Spirit, went on to preach, teach, and heal with supernatural ability.

So now it's your turn, Anointed Child of God! What can YOU do? Anything, because you are anointed and filled by God's Spirit to do the impossible.

Personal Study (15 minutes)

READ ROMANS 12:3–8, 1 CORINTHIANS 13, AND EPHESIANS 4:11–16. Let's do something a little different today. Remember how we talked about Paul's Holy Spirit GIFT LIST in our teaching session? Well, let's take a look at that list—which is spread out across these three passages of Scripture. Take a few moments to list the gifts given to the New Testament believers because of the Holy Spirit's presence among them.

What stands out to you?

What gifts do you have or wish you had?

I want to live a life empowered to do what God has called me to do, in very natural and supernatural ways.—**Bianca**

HOLY SPIRIT PERSPECTIVES. During session five, we talked about the different ways we can experience the Holy Spirit's presence in our lives: by knowing, seeing, feeling, and hearing. Think about your own life. Which of these seems to be the most common way you have experienced the power and the presence of the Holy Spirit? Write down a few words to make note of the stories that come to mind. If you tend to experience God in one particular area of life more than others, write down a few words or stories from your community. How have they experienced the Holy Spirit in these areas?

KNOW (OR SENSE):

SEE:

FEEL:

HEAR:

In the last days, God says, I will pour out my Spirit on all people. Your sons and daughters will prophesy, your young men will see visions, your old men will dream dreams. **—Acts 2:17**

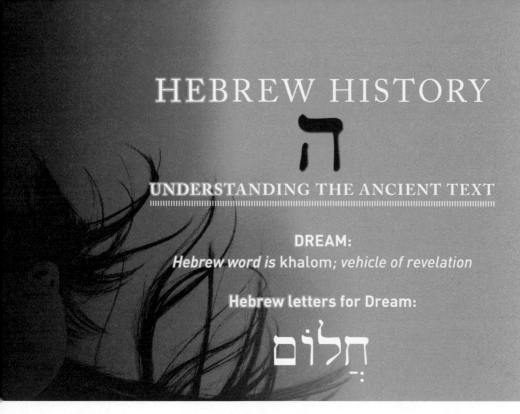

HEBREW HISTORY

UNDERSTANDING THE ANCIENT TEXT

DREAM:
Hebrew word is khalom; *vehicle of revelation*

Hebrew letters for Dream:

חֲלוֹם

Individual Prayer—Conversation with God

Use your own words to thank God for the ways He has shown Himself to you through knowing, seeing, feeling, and hearing. Thank God for the power of the Holy Spirit, who is always at work in you and around you, even when you're too busy to notice. Thank God that the same power of transformation shown in the fire and in the resurrection of Jesus is within you too.

Individual Activity (10 minutes)

Take some time today to be mindful of how, when, and where God is speaking to you through the Holy Spirit. You can use this space to document it, or write it in your journal, or even note it in your phone, but take time in your day to record where you sense the presence of God in your life. Then thank God for His Holy Spirit who is with you daily.

For where your treasure is, there will your heart be also.[13] —**Jesus**

Extra Credit (5 minutes)

We touched on the Holy Spirit during session five, but I want to dig a little deeper if you have the extra time today. Throughout the Old and New Testaments, we see and hear stories of people who knew (or sensed), saw, felt, and heard God. As you continue to think about this awareness, take note of how God is trying to get your attention. *Is it in His "usual" way with you? Or is it in a new way now that He has your full attention?*

What stands out to you about how these characters in the Bible experienced God?

GENESIS 37

1 SAMUEL 3

ACTS 9:1–9

He is the LORD; let him do what is good in his eyes.[14] —**The Priest Eli**

And the peace of God, which transcends all understanding, will guard your hearts and your minds in Christ Jesus. —**Philippians 4:7**

DAY FIVE
EMPOWERED

Not by Might Nor by Power

This is it. We are on our last day together, and no lie, my heart kind of aches. I know we are far away from each other, perhaps we've never even met, but my mind and heart are with you. If you've journeyed the last five weeks with me, then you are probably at some point in life where you want transformation to occur. I've been there. And so have many characters in the Bible who cried out to God for their situation to change.

But change and transformation, rebuilding and repairing, movement and momentum happen when God **does** it, not when we **force** it. Zechariah was a man in the Old Testament who received a word from the Lord that I want us to hold on to as we move forward in our lives: "'Not by might nor by power, but by my Spirit,' says the LORD Almighty" (Zechariah 4:6).

So cry out, and surrender, and hold on to the promises of God, and find great community, and allow the Holy Spirit to move ... then wait. Don't strive, don't punch the air, don't DO ... just BE. Be still and know that God is able to do exceedingly abundantly more than you can think or imagine—but it will be on His timeline, not yours.

Don't waver in weakness. Don't defer your destiny. Don't push for power. Wait like the apostles on the day of Pentecost in Acts 2. Wait for the Spirit of God to move in your life so radically that others will be amazed at the things God is doing in you, through you, and for you. Then boldly proclaim that it's not by your might or your power, but by God's Holy Spirit that you are being transformed.

Personal Study (15 minutes)

 READ EPHESIANS 3:14–20. Let's break this down. What stands out to you in this passage?

What does this passage say about each member of the Trinity: God the Father, Jesus Christ, and the Holy Spirit?

How does believing this passage change your perspective? How does it encourage your heart today?

I want to dare you to ask, "God, what do You want from me?" What do you sense God saying to you when you ask Him this question?

You are ABLE because of who God is.—**Bianca**

 READ JOHN 14:15–21. In this passage, Jesus is explaining how the promise of the Holy Spirit will become the presence of the Holy Spirit. Think about the early Christians of the New Testament and how confused or desperate they must have felt trying to figure out what Jesus was saying in this moment. He promised the presence of the Holy Spirit—a gift they would not understand until He was no longer with them. How would you answer these prompts in light of the early Christians and the presence of Holy Spirit with them after the death, resurrection, and ascension of Jesus?

- GOD HEARD:

- GOD REMEMBERED:

- GOD SAW:

- GOD KNEW:

Welcome the Holy Spirit into this moment with you. Ask God to empower you through the Holy Spirit in the following ways as you more forward from here:

- RELATIONALLY:

- SPIRITUALLY:

- PHYSICALLY:

- EMOTIONALLY:

Therefore go and make disciples of all nations, baptizing them in the name of the Father and of the Son and of the Holy Spirit.—**Matthew 28:19**

HEBREW HISTORY

UNDERSTANDING THE ANCIENT TEXT

POWER:
Hebrew word is toqeph*; authority, strength, energy*

Hebrew letters for the Power:

Individual Prayer—Conversation With God

Use your own words today to express to God whatever is on your heart in this moment. Thank God for the words He spoke to you, the understanding He gave to you, and the fire He lit within you over these last few study sessions. Invite God to transform your life as you surrender to His will, and ask Him to empower you with the Holy Spirit in this place.

Individual Activity (10 minutes)

This is our last activity together, and since we won't be spending daily time together in God's Word, my heart is that you delve DEEP into God's Word on your own. We all live busy lives, but consecrate—set apart—time for you to be with God and hear Him speak to you through His Word.

It might feel overwhelming to read the Bible, but do it piece-by-piece, verse-by-verse. If you want help, here are a few ideas. First, **decide** where you are going to start. I loooooooove reading the Bible in order so I have a full scope of the narrative. For example, if you read the book of James, start with James 1:1. Next, **read** the passage (the full chapter or even just one verse), and maybe even write it down in your journal or notebook to help you remember it. **Think** about what you just read. **Pray** that God would give you insight to what He wants to show you. Finally, **apply** what you read to your life.

We don't have to make things feel so academic. Just enter your time with God and ask for Him to reveal Himself through His Word. My greatest happiness would be that you would fall in love with God's holy Word and experience Him through the pages of Scripture.

We need to have faith in order to keep moving forward.—**Bianca**

Extra Credit (5 minutes)

We touched on the Holy Spirit in session five, but I want to dig a little deeper if you have the extra time today. I know you may still have a lot of questions about the manifestation of the Holy Spirit, or the gifts of the Holy Spirit, or the Trinity. I do too! But what we do know about the Holy Spirit is what we learn from Scripture.

Take a few moments to read through one more passage on the Holy Spirit in Romans 8. *What do these particular verses tell you about life through the Spirit?*

ROMANS 8:2

ROMANS 8:5–6

ROMANS 8:14

He is faithful to transform us in the fire.—**Bianca**

BENEDICTION

Now to him who is able to do immeasurably more than all we ask or imagine, according to his power that is at work within us, to him be glory in the church and in Christ Jesus throughout all generations, for ever and ever! Amen.
—Ephesians 3:20–21

When I was a little girl, our associate pastor used this verse to close out every sermon he preached. It was his benediction—his blessing on us, to us, and for us—on those Sundays. So this is it! My benediction for you. The end of your study guide, the end of my lame jokes, and the closing of our time together.

My hope for you is that you walk out of this experience a different person than when you walked in. May you have the courage to **cry out** to God, **surrender** to Him, remember His **promises**, find strength in **community**, and feel **empowered** by the Holy Spirit as you step out of your comfort zone into the fire. The past is in your past for a reason! God is inviting you to move forward and be transformed by His presence and by His work deep within you. He's inviting you to PLAY WITH FIRE.

XO,

YOUR COMMITMENT

What do you hope to get out of this study? Tell God, not me!

Your Signature _____

ENDNOTES

THE STORY OF THE PHOENIX

1. Adapted from "The Story of the Phoenix," *The Phoenix: Legends, Stories, and Poems*, http://www.phoenixarises.com/phoenix/legends/story.htm.

SESSION ONE: CRYING OUT

1. Chuck DeGroat, "Three Truths About the 'Dark Night of the Soul,'" *Christianity Today*, February 23, 2015, http://www.christianitytoday.com/le/2015/february-online-only/3-truths-of-dark-night-of-soul.html.

2. Dr. Seuss, *Oh, The Places You'll Go!* (New York: Random House, 1990).

3. 2 Corinthians 12:10.

4. "Ember," *Merriam-Webster's Dictionary*, http://www.merriam-webster.com/dictionary/ember.

5. Jeremiah 33:3.

6. Bianca Olthoff, Hebrew word definitions from video teaching notes, *Play with Fire* video sessions (2016).

7. Psalm 55:1–2.

8. Olthoff, *Play with Fire* (Grand Rapids: Zondervan, 2016), pp. 39–40.

9. Psalm 107:2, 6.

10. Olthoff, *Play with Fire*, p. 54.

11. Jeremiah 30:2.

12. Exodus 3:7.

13. Olthoff, *Play with Fire*, p. 187–188.

14. Psalm 139:1.

SESSION TWO: SURRENDER

1. Bianca Olthoff, *Play with Fire* (Grand Rapids: Zondervan, 2016), pp. 97–100.

2. Psalm 37:7.

3. Olthoff, *Play with Fire*, pp. 52–58.

4. Colossians 1:9.

5. Romans 8:31.

6. Olthoff, *Play with Fire*, pp. 148–154.

7. Bianca is chief storyteller for the A21 Campaign. See www.a21.org.

8. 2 Corinthians 1:10–11 MSG.

SESSION THREE: GOD'S PROMISES

1. Bianca Olthoff, *Play with Fire* (Grand Rapids: Zondervan, 2016), pp. 21–22.

2. Ibid., pp. 124–125.

3. Exodus 14:14.

4. Olthoff, *Play with Fire*, pp. 130–131.

5. Psalm 119:130.

6. John 14:4.

7. Exodus 15:13.

8. Joshua 23:6.

9. Olthoff, *Play with Fire*, pp. 145–146.

10. Ibid., p. 155.

11. Hebrews 3:13 MSG.

12. Psalm 119:125.

13. Olthoff, *Play with Fire*, pp. 162–163.

14. Philippians 4:9.

15. Exodus 3:12.

16. Psalm 119:11.

17. Ezekiel 36:27.

SESSION FOUR: COMMUNITY

1. Bianca Olthoff, *Play with Fire* (Grand Rapids: Zondervan, 2016), pp. 135–136.

2. Ibid. pp. 59–60.

3. Ibid, pp. 140–141.

4. Dan Britton, Jimmy Page, and Jon Gordon, *One Word That Will Change Your Life* (New York: John Wiley & Sons, 2012).

5. 1 John 3:1.

6. Olthoff, *Play with Fire*, pp. 35–36.

7. Deuteronomy 31:8

8. Matthew 18:20.

9. Acts 4:32.

10. Olthoff, *Play with Fire*, pp. 169–170.

11. Psalm 62:1.

12. 1 Corinthians 3:13.

13. Olthoff, *Play with Fire*, pp. 142–143.

14. Daniel 3:29.

15. Exodus 33:18.

16. Romans 12:18.

SESSION FIVE: HOLY SPIRIT

1. Bianca Olthoff, *Play with Fire* (Grand Rapids: Zondervan, 2016), pp. 83–86.

2. Corrie ten Boom, with Elizabeth Sherrill and John Sherrill, *The Hiding Place* (Grand Rapids: Chosen Books, 2006).

3. Olthoff, *Play with Fire*, pp. 85–86.

4. Ibid., p. 146.

5. Ibid., pp. 89–90.

6. Joel 2:28.

7. 1 Timothy 2:1.

8. "Intercession," *Merriam-Webster's Dictionary*, http://www.merriam-webster.com/dictionary/intercession.

9. Romans 12:6.

10. Olthoff, *Play with Fire*, pp. 93–94.

11. Luke 2:37.

12. John 4:48.

13. Matthew 6:21.

14. 1 Samuel 3:18.

Play with Fire

Discovering Fierce Faith, Unquenchable Passion, and a Life-Giving God

Bianca Juárez Olthoff

Play with Fire, the debut book by popular speaker and teacher Bianca Juárez Olthoff, is the reminder that God isn't waiting until you have more resources or a spouse or a job so he can use you. He's ready to use you now.

Using the mythical creature, the Phoenix, which was also referenced by early church leaders, she parallels this story with God's work in her own life, highlighting the beauty of reinvention with fire as both the impetus and the method for change. Olthoff reminds us that we serve a God who is redemptive and can take the worst situations and use them for His glory.

Play with Fire is a Bible-infused message that will help women discover:

- The way out of the middle is moving forward
- The personal and powerful nature of the Holy Spirit
- The power and sacrifice of transformation
- The unique calling and purpose of life involves transformation

With Olthoff's distinct style, strong storytelling gifts, and powerful Bible teaching, *Play with Fire* will remind readers that God has huge dreams for them. In Bianca's words, "He's whispering in the wind and speaking through the fire and shouting in silence the extraordinary dream He is birthing in you. His dream for you is far greater than the dream you have for yourself. It's not your identity or income or influence that will make this happen. Like Zechariah 4:6 says, 'It's not by might nor by power, but by my Spirit,' says the Lord." It's time to play with fire.

Available in stores and online!

EVERY 30 SECONDS

somebody is forced into the
bondage of modern-day slavery.
We exist to change that.

———————————————

Our goal for humanity is simple: Freedom.

Join us as we work to abolish injustice in the 21st century.

A21.org   @A21   @A21   @A21